THE MINISTRY OF BRANDING

A BIBLICAL APPROACH TO BRAND BUILDING FOR MINISTRY

MIKE MARTIN

For bulk ordering or booking: www.meetmikemartin.com, www.theministryofbranding.com

ISBN: 9781720179009

Cover Art By: JLynn Stemley
Interior Layout By: Michael S. Martin II
Edited By: Cy'Ress Cade
Final Edits By: Ricky Watson Jr.

In Memory of my father,
Michael S. Martin Sr.

The greatest inheritance you ever gave me was your name. You lived your life as a man committed to God, your family and beyond reproach. You were the greatest example of manhood. I pray that I carry it in honor of the great man that you were. I will do my best to wear the brand well. Love you always.

In Memory of my mother,
Yvonne D. Martin

At an extremely young age you empowered me to be creative. You introduced me to the business world and allowed me to experiment with branding and marketing your businesses. You believed in me more than I believed in myself. You were my number one cheer leader. Your pride in me has been my motivation. I miss you dearly.
Love,
Your Son, aka Boyda

Dedicated to my sister,
Crystal Martin.

Thanks for thinking greatly of me and supporting me in every endeavor. You are my creative twin, business partner and sidekick.

Dedicated to My spiritual father,

Matthew L. Stevenson III

You are the reason this book exists. Your life and your selfless love and investment, has pulled so much purpose out of me, that I will never be the same. I am forever thankful that I met a prophet at the well. I can't imagine who I would be without you. It is an honor to be a son. Thank you! Thank you! Thank you!

Special thanks to...

Apostle Raleigh Mayberry

You have been an activator, an inspiration, a leader, a brother and a friend. Thank you for pushing me and believing in me. I appreciate you!

My Church Family

All Nations Worship Assembly - Thank you for supporting me always.

The Prophets

Arian Johnson, John Umunna, Ryan Booker and Gabby Hopson, thank you so for consistently praying for me during one of the most difficult seasons of my life. Your calls, office visits, text messages and spiritual direction for this book, were of great strength to me.

My best friends Joseph Smith Jr. and Keith Strong.

For encouraging me on this journey.

And

My launch team.

Juliah Marley, Deonna Thompson, Jermany Thomas, Evan Brown, Michael Weatherspoon, Alan Fudge, Etienne Nelson, Eddie Sanders, Ken Daly, Jasmine Finley and Danny Marshall, your encouragement and you support is beyond value. Cy'Ress, thanks for calming my mind, with your edits to my writing. Ricky Watson, thanks for pushing me to write and for your final edits and critical eye. JLynn Stemley you are a genius thank you for helping me communicate my vision, like only you can.

Who Should Read This Book

The content of this book is primarily targeted to churches and ministry organizations. However, every person, business and organization can benefit from an effective branding strategy. With that in mind, this book will be a resource to pastors, church leaders, business owners, nonprofit organizations and anyone looking to improve their personal brand.

You don't have to be a business or marketing professional to read this book. This book was created with the novice in mind and includes exercises and steps to make the process of brand build as simple and easy to apply, as possible. No matter if you have just started your own jewelry making business or are launching a church, you need to reach an audience. You can't afford to start a business without taking the time to build your brand.

Chapter one will give you a general understand of branding and chapter two will reinforce the importance of branding, by providing biblical references to brand building. From there, you will embark on a brand strategy journey. This book is intended to be a reference manual that you can refer to from time to time.

About the Author

Mike Martin is a communicator, strategist and brand specialist with over 12 years of experience.

He works with national teams in the private and public sectors to build and improve their brands. As both a pastor and a marketing professional, he describes his work as creative ministry. His passion is helping ministries express their kingdom assignment through strategic brand identity. Over his career he has worked with large and small organizations to improve their branding, including the Chicago Housing Authority and All Nations Worship Assembly (ANWA), where he currently serves as the Executive Pastor and Chief Operating Officer.

In his full-time role, Mike is responsible for the ministry's communications such as brand development, public relations and creative direction. Prior to his work at ANWA, Mike Martin held a successful career as a Marketing Communications Consultant for several national public-sector agencies. His branding work is nationally recognized and he has even been acknowledged for his innovation in design by the Chicago Innovation Awards. With a degreed education in Graphic Design and Marketing Communications, Mike brings both a creative and executive aptitude to every project that he lends his skill.

To learn more about Mike Martin or to book him for a training workshop, visit *www.meetmikemartin.com*.

Contents

"*Without right presentation, there is no passion, and if there be no passion, there is no endurance!*"

– Dr. Matthew L. Stevenson III, Founder of the All Nations Worship Assembly
Global Church Network

Foreword

Presentation is powerful. In our culture, so much of who we are, what we think and what we believe is based upon presentation. God is a God of presentation. From Genesis to Revelation, The Holy Spirit, presents us with the keys to life, health, wealth, posterity and progress through the power of presentation. Unfortunately, through bad doctrine, abusive teaching and pure negligence, one of the things we have lost as the body of Christ, is the power of presentation. There is an unbreakable relationship between presentation and belief. Through presentation, we have the power to create belief.

In this book, Michael Martin, literally gives language to a FRESH paradigm for ministry in the 21st Century. He gives hope and proof that persuasion is possible and can be done through branding. He gives strong detail about how BRANDING, MARKETING and STRATEGIC COMMUNICATION is essential for the future of The Local Church. He is brilliant in his ideology and gives candid framework for how and why "Branding is Biblical".

In my own ministry, over the last 18 years, I have done the dance between appeal and compromise. Michael's mind has helped me realize that something can be appealing and not sinful. This literary classic breaks through the jargon, tradition and ignorance, that has blinded an entire generation of the opportunity we have in cities. We are afforded these opportunities through powerful, creative, and assertive branding.

I am not only proud of Michael's life and testimony, I am PROUD OF THIS BOOK. This book is destined to become a must read for anyone doing something new FOR the Kingdom. Without right presentation, there is no passion, and if there be no passion, there is no endurance! BRANDING IS BIBICAL, so let's be better at it.

Dr. Matthew L. Stevenson III, *Global Senior Pastor*
All Nations Worship Assembly, *Global*

Introduction

I grew up in church all my life. My family has a long lineage of ministers, pastors and preachers. Growing up, church for me was an integral in my life as school was. It wasn't an option. While many of my school mates were going to sports games and enjoying the weather on Sunday afternoons, I was in church. With a father who doubled as the church drummer and a minister and a mother who was a Sunday school teacher, I spent long hours in church. We would be in church on Sundays for nearly eight hours, not to mention the other week night events and services. It wasn't until I was an adult, when I realized that I didn't just grow up in church, church was my life. However, it was a life that I was completely happy with. I grew a love and appreciation not just for the institution of church, but also for the people that make up the church and the God that we gathered in church to worship. This passion was so deep that I would tell everyone that I would be a pastor one day.

After the unexpected death of my father, I wanted nothing to do with the church. Although I didn't blame God, the passion and the love that I had for the church began to dwindle. I later went away to college to study graphic design and marketing. Subsequently, the passion that I had for the church and for the bible was replaced by my new love for art, strategy and business. I no longer had a desire to be a pastor. I wanted to become a successful businessman with the talent and skill to make any business grow. As my business experiences and environments changed and developed, I grew a disgust for how church and consequently God was presented. This aversion caused me to attend church less frequently. The friends that were all church kids were now replaced by artists, creatives and entrepreneurs who believed in a God and a power. They just didn't believe that He dwelled in such shabby environments as many of the storefront churches in Chicago. I also began to take on this viewpoint. The Kingdom of God had to be bigger than the presentations that I saw on Sunday morning.

After college I spent several years in the business world, working fulltime as a marketing professional for a few companies and agencies. I also freelanced, as a graphic designer and marketing strategist for a few companies. I enjoyed the ability to present quality products and offerings in a way that showed the world how great they were. My work became nationally recognized and I thrived off of improving businesses and brands. I loved this new world so much that I planned to do it for the rest of my life, with a goal to never be a part of an institutionalized church again. In my mind, the church was no longer relevant as was only used by God to get His message out. I believed that it was no longer a requirement for the modern world. After all, we had the internet and digital bibles to research God. We didn't need a man in a pulpit to dictate and direct us.

I was headed astray but God scheduled a plot twist. After a vacationing with my sister and a few friends, all of whom were also "de-churched" adults, we all found ourselves visiting a small church on the southside of Chicago, called All Nations Worship Assembly. We knew nothing about the church or its pastor. From our hotel room, a few days before, my friend Ericka saw a friend of hers "check-in" to the church on Facebook. This prompted a brief discussion about church and our visit the following Sunday was our last ditch effort to give church a try.

It wasn't long into the service that I encountered the God of my childhood. The worship songs, the people and the teaching all resembled my church foundation. Throughout the service I found myself weeping in repentance for walking away from "The House of God." I even kneeled down on the floor of this dusty former synagogue, in my expensive business suit and I didn't care. I just wanted to regain the relationship with God that I once knew. This church which had nicknamed itself "The Well," was truly a place of refreshing.

As if I wasn't already sold on my need to return to God and His church, the pastor (Dr. Matthew Stevenson), whom I had never previously met, climbed across five rows of people and chairs to get to me. Once he reached me, he grabbed my head and prophesied things that I experienced that could have only been revealed to him, by God. His words reminded me how much God loved me and didn't care about mistakes I had made. He only desired for me to return home. I was a wreck.

The next Sunday, I returned with my friends. By the third visit, we were all walking down the aisle to return to Christ and make All Nations Worship Assembly, our new church home.

After eight months of conversation about my life story and walking me through the deliverance process, Dr. Stevenson made me the Executive Pastor and Creative Director of the ministry. I found great excitement and fulfillment in merging my knowledge of the business world with the power and presence of God, that was evident in each service at All Nations. Dr. Stevenson and I went on a rebrand journey of the entire ministry. We updated everything from the logo, website, the sanctuary carpet, stage and lighting. Within four years, that eight hundred member church that changed the course of my life, now has over five thousand members, a large online following and over six additional locations worldwide. We were intentional about our strategy and the presentation of the Kingdom and God breathed upon it. A brand of ministry was developed that made it easy for people to encounter God.

Churches, ministries, organizations and businesses must acknowledge that we live in a branded world. There is a fight for the attention and passions of people. In order to stand out in an overstimulated culture, the excellence of the Kingdom must be demonstrated and displayed with careful attention and strategy. It is important that organizations that endeavor to thrive, create branded touchpoints that appeal to the senses, attract, build and maintain a following.

Jesus was the perfect model for building a brand that will last for generations. He was intentional about the brand ambassadors that He selected and trained on the presentation of His brand. Even the mission and vision of His brand was announced and was clear. The Jesus brand gives us a clear blueprint strategy for branding any entity. It we look into the biblical template for branding, we will be much more closer to finding the success in our organizational efforts.

I tossed around several name choices when writing this book. It was important to me that the title on the outside accurately reflected the content on the inside. After several other choices that didn't stick, The Ministry of Branding, stood out. After all, branding is ministry work as much as the Sunday vocalist. They both ultimately intend to bring the audience closer to God. This book is filled with strategies to help you do just that.

Avoid the temptation to skip chapters. Even if you think you already have an understanding of the subject matter, read every chapter. There may be tips or information that may enhance your brand strategy. Even if you already have an existing brand, complete each of the exercises they will help to strengthen your brand. Once you have finished the entire book, refer back to it and use it as a reference tool. A brand is a living breathing entity. It doesn't stop with the completion of this book. It must be monitored and reviewed regularly to ensure its health and growth.

I make no guarantees that your organization will experience the same growth that I have experienced with my work. No matter how you dress the packaging, the content inside the package still has to have great quality to inspire repeat interactions from the consumer. It is my hope that this book helps you to start the journey of brand development. After this lengthy preamble, it's time to start your journey.

"Your brand is what people say about you when you're not in the room."

– Jeff Bezos, Founder of Amazon.com

1
Understanding Branding

Intentional brand building is relatively new to the church world. In many cases, it is still considered taboo. Often, religious people and organizations have wrongly associated branding with secularism and salesmanship. They fear that branding ministry somehow dilutes the power and move of the Spirit. Some would even say, "You can't brand the Bride of Christ, God has already done that!" These are grossly erroneous perceptions of branding.

I could attribute the Church's misconceptions of intentional branding to several factors, but I think two of the primary reasons people fight against branding is: (1) that they do not realize how important branding is to God and (2) that they do not understand the real definition of branding. At the risk of sounding overly spiritual, I must say that the fear of branding must be overcome and the myths about branding must be dispelled, if the church is to ever live beyond a postmodern world and have influence in the lives of people.

Branding Ministry is not about selling Church – it's about illustrating who the Church is. The goal of this chapter is to, in essence, "rebrand ministry branding."

What is a Brand?

Maybe the easiest way to define a "**brand**" is to start by explaining what a brand is not. A brand is not a logo, it's not a slogan, it's not a color scheme or a name. One of the most common inaccuracies people make when defining a brand is listing the bricks that build a brand. A brand is more than the summation of its parts. While logos and colors help to construct your brand, they are not your brand. These things are just **brand visuals**.

To use brand components to define a brand is like defining a person by their attire. If you were to ask a person who knows me, *"Who is Michael?"* You would be a little confused if they said, *"He is a black t-shirt."* I may be wearing a black t-shirt and it may even be a t-shirt that I wear all the time however, the t-shirt does not give you an accurate definition of who I am. Who I am as a person is defined by my character. Brands are defined in a similar way. Like people, brands have a name, a personality and a reputation.

> **All brands live in the minds of people and are built on previous experiences.**

A **brand** is an experience that people have when they encounter a business, product, service, organization or church. These customer experiences are what reflect a ministry's unique personality and character. These experiences, good and bad, are what people will share with others. Over time, they become the definition of your brand. Great logos, colors and slogans don't overshadow poor brand experiences. The experiences people have, form the opinions and the words people use to describe your ministry. Founder of Amazon.com, Jeff Bezos said it best; *"Your brand is what people say about you when you are not in the room."*

What are people saying about your brand when they don't know that you are listening?

Brands are not tangible. All brands live in the minds of people and are built on previous experiences. Those thoughts are the basis of your brand. For a church or a ministry, your brand is how people feel when they leave your church service or conference. What do your church attendees or members say to their friends and family when asked, *"How was the service?"*

A few questions that will explain your ministry's brand are:

> *"What did you like most about the service?"*
> *"What didn't you like about the service?"*
> *"What stood out most?"*
> and most important… *"How did the service make you feel?"*

The answers to these questions will provide you with a picture and an understanding of what people think of your brand or service. Although these questions are specific to ministries, they would apply to other organizations as well.

If your ministry is currently in operation, I recommend that you survey your members and first-time guests by asking them the series of questions listed above. The answers to those questions will identify your brand. They explain the thoughts that come to mind when people hear your ministry's name. You may be shocked by the responses that you receive. When you ask those questions, you must resist the urge to defend your brand. Hear them, consider them and find ways to improve them, to help shape your brand.

Realizing Brand Value

Strong brands can last for generations. Even during recessions, brands like Coca-Cola, Mercedes Benz and McDonalds survive. This principle was proved true during the Global Financial Crisis of 2008: brands like Walmart and Amazon not only survived but increased their **Market Share**. The reason these businesses and businesses like them last and survive when other companies fold, is a direct result of their **Brand Value**.

Brand Value or Brand Equity is the value that a brand holds in the marketplace. To put it simply, a highly-valued brand (a brand with high equity) means that the brand is recognized by more people for positive offerings than any other business or organization, in its category. This means that your brand is the first one that people think of when they think of your industry. It also means that the brand is easily recognizable when seen in an advertisement.

Two brands that have worldwide brand value are Coca-Cola and McDonalds. These brands are recognized by more people, globally for their offerings. Coca-Cola is the first company recalled when you ask people about soda companies. When most people think of fast food, McDonalds is often the first company to come to mind. Even if your impressions of these companies are not the best, they hold a level of brand recognition that exceed that of their competitors.

At the most basic level, brand value is customer brand knowledge.

Take a moment and think about where your church or organization falls in the rankings when asked about your industry locally. Now expand that ranking to statewide and then nationally.

How many people would recommend your church when asked, "What is a good church to attend in your city?"

Now the equity comes into play when you consider how much people are willing to pay for the product or service that your brand offers. Individuals would be willing to pay a premium to be associated with brands that have a high brand value. For example; the Air Jordan 10 reportedly cost Nike a little more than $16.00 per pair to make. These same shoes listed for resale ranging from $250.00 to $550.00 per pair, depending on color and size. Companies like Nike and the Jordan Brand have achieved such high brand value that people are willing to pay as much as 34 times the amount it costs to make them. This value is so important that a company with a high brand value will be worth more than its **Book Value**, when you consider the intangible asset of its brand equity.

When you integrate purpose in your branding, you communicate purpose in your church.

At the most basic level, brand value is customer brand knowledge. It is the awareness that your brand holds in the minds of your customers. You are the creator of your brand's value because you are responsible for your church's branding. Every organization should protect and invest in its brand equity because the returns can be residual, when done correctly.

What is Branding?

A "brand" is different from "Branding." **Branding** is the process of crafting the experiences and images you desire for people to have and remember when encountering your organization. It is the development of an organization's identity. This is where the word "intentional" comes into play. In order to properly build a brand experience the intentional actions of a ministry, to build a brand experience, are what shapes the thoughts and opinions people have about your brand. When you integrate purpose in your branding, you communicate purpose in your church and/ or organization.

Branding is cumulative. It is built over time with thousands of small interactions. Branding is not just one good or bad experience. A mantra that my team and I live by is, "everything communicates." When a person walks into our church the communicative factors are: the smell, the lighting, the location of restrooms, the friendliness of the greeters and ushers, even the color of the paint on the walls. From the moment, a person walks into your church, these elements are screaming, *"This is who we are!"*

A relationship is formed when customers interact with your brand. There are several ways that people interact with your brand: when they visit your website, when they are ushered to their seats, when they give via the mobile app or when they receive an email.

Your brand exists to solve a problem in a person's life and to make them feel a certain way when they encounter it. The way that you want them to feel when they interact with your church is your

Brand Personality. If you aren't intentional about branding your organization, people will brand it for you. They will determine the adjectives that describe your brand and those words will reflect how they interact with your offerings. The way to avoid poor brand representation is to establish a brand personality in a way that not only beats them to the punch but is strong enough to bypass any unintended descriptions and emotions.

Take a moment to review Table 1.1 below. The first column in the table lists sample adjectives that may describe an organization and the second column lists sample feelings that you may want your customer to feel when encountering your brand.

Table 1.1 **Brand Adjectives and Feelings**

Adjectives	Feelings
• Progressive	• Motivated
• Relevant	• Encouraged
• Transformative	• Changed
• Orthodox	• Empowered
• Traditional	• Equipped
• Practical	• Enlightened
• Fresh	• Victorious
• Communal	• Renewed
• Powerful	• Rejuvenated
• Inspiring	• Excited

Now use this table to start on a plan to draft the adjectives that describe your brand and the feelings you desire for people to have, when they encounter your brand. You can use some of the words that I have listed, but also try to come up with some of your own. Once you have selected your brand words, you will have a solid foundation to construct and grow your brand.

The Goal of Branding

Intentionally shaping what people think and believe when they think of you is the ultimate goal of "branding.". We have established that a brand is not a logo or a color but the process of branding or designing a brand identity may include the use of these components to communicate who you are. In the heavy media-driven age that we live in, first impressions last. Your brand can either bring people closer to God or push them further away.

A brand should fulfill a certain set of criteria to be memorable and attractive in a person's mind. This set of criteria varies depending on the audience and their predisposition. The way a brand presents itself should have purpose. This principle should be increasingly evident in the branding of ministry. Branding requires a vision from the senior leadership and an eagerness to invest in the future.

Engaging in branding is to establish long term strategy for defining who you are. Branding is translating a pre-planned message into clear and direct communication. It is the ability to adjust and manage how people perceive you, by helping to define their connection with you and ultimately – God. A great brand accurately communicates who the ministry is and establishes trust and loyalty. Branding is taking your ministry's vision and incorporating it into every element that may influence a person's perception of your church. Effective branding has the ability to influence perception.

Perception Influence

We have established that a brand lives in the mind of the customer. Businesses and churches must consistently monitor current and potential customers to understand how their brand is perceived. These perceptions are shared and communicated to their community. Perception is how people feel about a thing and how they see a thing in relationship to themselves.

Perception was important to Jesus. Scripture illustrates several times where Jesus perceived the thoughts of people and re-communicated to ensure that they were perceiving Him the way He wanted them to perceive Him. He even did and said things for the benefit of the perception of others. In John 11:41-42, Jesus' prayer at the tomb of Lazarus was for the perception and understanding of the people. As He prayed, He said, *"I knew that you always listen to me, but I said this for the sake of the crowd standing around here, that they may believe that you sent me."* THIS is branding and the management of brand perception!

The success of a brand depends on how it is perceived. Studies have shown that almost half of **Brand Perception** is attributed to *what* organizations say and *how* they say it. The other half may be the result of a customer's direct contact with an organization, it's product or service. Combining messaging and interactions will influence a customer's perception of your brand. When managed properly, positive brand perception will attract people to your church, business or organization.

Awareness of how your brand is perceived establishes consistency in messaging and cultivates brand trust.

Without knowing how people perceive your brand, effective marketing and the growing of your organization will be difficult, if not impossible. Awareness of how your brand is perceived establishes consistency in messaging and cultivates brand trust. Scripture teaches us in 1 Samuel 16:7 that it is the nature of man to judge the outward appearance. Those judgements stem from what people see, hear and, often times from the status they hold. These things must be considered when you are brand building.

Brand perception doesn't have to be a mystery. By employing monitoring-activities such as surveying your target audience, you can better understand how people see your church and initiate effort towards change. A **Target Audience** is a specific group of people, identified as the intended recipients of a message.

At All Nations Worship Assembly, where I serve as the Executive Pastor and the Director of Operations and Communication, I hired a Social Media Manager. This individual's full-time job is to not only post content to all of our social media accounts, but he is also responsible for monitoring and responding to parishioners reviews. He responds to the good and bad reviews. When people comment with a complaint about the church or the service, he apologizes on behalf of the church and informs them that we have taken their complaint into consideration. This takes our social media accounts from being just another community calendar or advertising board and makes it more personable. Every response, or lack of response communicates the brand.

We must perceive a thing, to believe in its authenticity. In this culture, seeing is believing. We are inundated with so many images and pictures, that we have grown to rely on these things, as our foundation, when it pertains to trusting a brand. We must perceive a thing, to believe in its authenticity. Just as Jesus displayed several actions, solely for the perception of others, churches must display the images that they desire for people to perceive. If a church desires to attract a multicultural congregation, people must see a multicultural leadership team. If people are to believe in the prosperity of the Christian life, then it must be authentically revealed in the lives of the members and not just the senior pastor.

If you want people to believe that you are a youthful church, then you must have youth in the forefront. Every area of your church must authentically display the image that you want people to believe.

You Have a Brand: Even if You Don't Know it

Whether you planned for it or not, your church already has a brand. Every staff hire, carpet choice, web design, color selection, etc. helps to communicate the character of your church. Everything expresses your brand.

The church with no children's ministry communicates, "We don't want families here." The church with pastel carpet and walls communicates, "We are a church for women. Men are not welcome." The church with overgrown grass and dirty windows communicates, "We don't value God's house, so neither should you." EVERYTHING COMMUNICATES.

To define your church's brand, you must establish systems and guidelines that assist in making decisions that best represent who you really are and what you desire to communicate. This means considering your brand in everything, down to the uniform of your hosts and ushers.

One of the best illustrations of this is in 1 Kings 10, when the Queen of Sheba came to meet King Solomon for the first time.

> "And when the queen of Sheba had seen all the wisdom of Solomon, the house that he had built, the food on his table, the seating of his servants, the service of his waiters and their apparel, his cupbearers, and his entryway by which he went up to the house of the Lord, there was no spirit in her. Then she said to the king: 'It was a true report which I heard in my own land about your words and your wisdom."
>
> 1 Kings 10:4-6

Everything in Solomon's temple was evidence of the reality of God's work. The order, structure, customer service and the design of his entryways professed to the evidence of God. Before King Solomon said one word to her, his brand communicated who he was and created perception in the mind of the queen. His branding brought deliverance to the queen. As a first-time visitor, the queen looked on the outside and concluded that God is real.

The king had a brand, managed the perception of his brand and influenced the faith of the queen. If it worked for King Solomon, it will work for your ministry today.

Take a moment and think about how your church is displaying its brand. Before the choir sings and before the sermon is delivered, what brand elements are visible? What are those brand elements communicating? Will the faith of your first-time visitors increase because of your brands communication?

Why is Branding Important for Ministry?

A brand is an expression of the spiritual vocation of your church.

For any business, the brand is one of their most important assets. In the case of ministry, the brand is a representation of Christ and an expression of the spiritual vocation of your church. Branding becomes the face of your mission. Successful branding will widen your influence and expand your reach.

Ministries and churches have huge walls to scale when attempting to reach their target audiences. These walls are generally built because of negative church experiences. Once a person receives an invitation to return to church, the first thing that comes to mind is their previously established perception. Ministries must be intentional about branding beyond those previous encounters and recoloring their pallet for church, specifically your church and ultimately God.

Planning an attractive, clear and consistent brand isn't about trying to make the church secular; however, it is about removing barriers to entry for new believers. As we said before, people already have their preconceived ideas and expectations of church, whether good or bad. When branding for ministry, you must brand beyond the heart, the mind and the will to reach the spirit. These layers of invisible barriers to communication must be overcome by great preaching and teaching, visual branding and people interactions.

Effective branding must:

> brand beyond the heart to… *establish trust.*
> brand beyond the mind to… *establish legitimacy.*
> brand beyond the will to… *establish desire.*

Branding Beyond the Heart:

When considering your branding, many people have already had bad experiences with churches and church people. Often, people feel judged or misunderstood, which has caused them to build walls against the church to protect their hearts. They may even see "church people" as a bunch of hypocrites. The brand and the church must be presented as a group of imperfect but authentic people serving a perfect God. To effectively reach these individuals, churches must build brands that people can relate to. Many people have had at least a few positive life experiences, which means there is some common ground. Personalities differ but the beauty of shared experiences help us to relate and establish trust. This trust breaks down the barrier to the heart.

Branding Beyond the Mind:

Another experience barrier is the mind. The current generation of millennials are known as the most educated generation of our time. According to a report released in 2014 by The Council of Economic Advisers to President Obama, 47 percent of 25 to 34-year-olds received a postsecondary degree and an additional 18 percent had completed some postsecondary education. As this generation and generations following them continue to expand in knowledge, they rationalize themselves out of church and religion. Many people in this generation view the Church not only as archaic, but also as socially unaware. If an unbeliever has intellectual disagreements with the Bible, slick talking and cliché preaching will not motivate them to genuine belief in God.

Churches and pastors must deliver the gospel and their brand beyond the barrier of the mind to establish legitimacy. This means delivering revelation of the Word beyond Sunday School basics and displaying that revelation by applying excellence to everything that is executed in the church.

Branding Beyond the Will:

Branding beyond the will means creating desire. One of the most powerful instruments in the orchestra of branding is connecting with a customer's desire. Desire is a powerful and compelling emotion that turns attraction into decision-making. Will and desire encourages a first-time visitor to take that intimidating walk down the aisle to the altar. Brands that evoke a strong connection with a customer's desire turns a want into a need. People will realize that they not only *want* to be a part of your church, but they *need* to be a part. Desirable brands lead to loyalty and endorsement. Much like the loyal Apple users, they identify with and desire Apple products so much, that they are not only customers, but they have become the brand's biggest ambassadors.

It should be the goal of every organization to design experiences that are memorable and impactful to the people they encounter.

Organizations should build brands that are not confined to religious sectors. Church brands should be recognized globally and able to compete with an Apple, Google or Starbucks for brand space in a person's mind. The problem is that many churches don't see the value in branding or are intimidated by the thought, effort and resources needed to do branding the right way.

When combined with strategic marketing and communications, strong ministry brands should attract, engage and retain believers.

It should be the goal of every church to design experiences that are memorable and impactful to the people they encounter. These brands should be able to last for generations. One common mistake that I have seen most churches make is branding their ministries around the senior pastor and not the ministry as a whole. The problem is most measurable when a pastor retires or passes away. Ministries that have not built a strong brand around the church do not last beyond the transition of leadership. When combined with strategic marketing and communications, strong ministry brands should attract, engage and retain believers. They also should last for generations. Generational longevity should be the goal.

The Trinity: Branding, Marketing, Communications

Branding, marketing and communications are terms frequently used interchangeably. While each of them work together, they each hold their own distinction; much like the Trinity. They are three in one. Maybe an easier way to visualize this idea is to look at "branding" as the product (the item), "marketing" as the process of shipping the product (the delivery truck) and "communications" as the packaging that describes the product inside (the box). You need all three to effectively deliver your product to the target audience.

Branding

Branding has already been established as the process of crafting the experiences and images you desire for people to have and remember when encountering your brand. It is the development of an organization's identity. "Who we are, what we do, and why we do what we do." Branding is the development of *The Item*. Now that you have developed this item, you need to get it to the recipient. This is where "marketing" comes into play.

Marketing

The American Marketing Association defines **Marketing** as exchanging offerings that have value for customers, clients, partners and society at large. Marketing is the overall strategy. In this phase, you are selecting the vehicles. This is when you determine the use of direct mail, websites, social media, billboards, flyers, brochures, television commercials, etc. It is how we get the product to where it is going. Now that you have selected your delivery truck, you now need to package the item to be delivered.

Communications

According to the National Communication Association, the discipline of communication focuses on how people use messages to generate meanings within and across various contexts, cultures, channels, and media. To simplify this complex definition, **Communications** is the creation of written content for your website, social media accounts and brochures. This process is the development of words and images that reach your target audience. Communications is the announcement of your ministry's benefits and features, similar to the descriptive text on the outside of the box that says *"100% Cotton"* or *"Completely Waterproof."*

A brand or branding is not a secular theory or need. It is the intentional clarification of who you are; the definition of your character. Shining a light on your best attributes and taking an interest in what people think of you should not be limited to the business world. Branding is important for ministry as well. Churches must realize that people who are not already familiar with their ministry should not be expected to know the intent of the pastor's heart. In order to ensure effective communication of who an organization is and what it stands for, careful attention must be given to branding.

Activity 1 *Adjectives and Feelings*	Draw a line down the center of a sheet of paper. On one side of the line, write a list of adjectives that you desire for your brand to be known for. On the other side, write a list of feelings that you want associated with your brand. Keep this list for use in other activities. Reference Table 1.1.

"But you are the ones chosen by God, chosen for the high calling of priestly work, chosen to be a holy people, God's instruments to do his work and speak out for him, to tell others of the night-and-day difference he made for you – from nothing to something, from rejected to accepted."

- 1 Peter 2:9-10 (MSG)

If you are a Christian who does not believe in branding ministry, then you might want to stop wearing a cross as jewelry or driving a car with the Christian symbol of a fish on the bumper. Believe it or not, both symbols are a form of branding. While the Bible does not instruct us to wear the cross as our necklaces and earrings, hang them on our walls or from our car's rear view mirrors, I do believe that He has permitted the cross to be a reminder of His brand and all that it represents. Even the Bible itself is one of the best and longest lasting brand identity guides. A **Brand Identity Guide** is the primary documentation of your company's brand. It gives direction and guidance on how a brand should be used internally and externally.

Like a Brand Identity Guide, the Bible tells the believer how to consistently represent God...

A brand identity guide ensures that your brand is focused on consistency, persistence, and restraint. Great brands are consistently represented, persistently communicated and adhere to certain restraints. Like a brand identity guide, the Bible tells the believer how to consistently represent God, to persistently communicate his message and to live a life under certain restraints to ensure that His message is not tainted. Clearly, God is the originator of branding.

In this chapter, I endeavor to explain biblical principles for branding and how you can incorporate the same principles into your ministry's brand. These are not guaranteed ways to grow your ministry or organization, but proper implementation of these principles should improve your effort and reach.

Is Branding Ministry Biblical?

Any branding professional will tell you that your brand should have a set of brand guidelines that establish the message (or story), a target audience and your brand voice. For the Bible, a clear representation of these brand guidelines is in the Ten Commandments. The Ten Commandments are ten guidelines or principles that govern Christianity. Subsequently, all Christian teachings stem from these core teachings.

To make it clear, let's look closer at one commandment that is a direct illustration of God's idea of branding. The third commandment is a well-known, but often misinterpreted part of the Bible. Growing up, I was always led to believe that this Scripture was about using profanity. While that may be a partial truth, the overarching truth is much bigger.

> Our job is to know Him and make Him known. However, there are standards for our vocation.

> *"You shall not misuse the name of the LORD your God, for the LORD will not hold anyone guiltless who misuses his name."*
>
> Exodus 20:7 (NIV)

This commandment is saying so much more than, *"Don't use my name when you swear."* The third commandment is God telling His people not to misrepresent His brand. God is very serious about protecting the brand. Just as a retailer is concerned about how the staff handles customer service and represents the company, God is concerned about how Christians represent His brand. We are to live lives that reflect His brand character and attributes. We are God's brand ambassadors. Although we can admit, we don't always represent His brand well, it is apparent that God expects us to go into the world to speak for Him and "persuade" others to live for Him, by telling our own stories of conversion. These stories are testimonies, or as they are referred to in the business world, "testimonials."

In the second chapter of 1 Peter, we are reminded of our assignment (or calling) and the privilege of our appointment.

> *But you are the ones chosen by God, chosen for the high calling of priestly work, chosen to be a holy people, God's instruments to do his work and speak out for him, to tell others of the night-and-day difference he made for you – from nothing to something, from rejected to accepted.*
>
> 1 Peter 2:9-10 (MSG)

Our job is to know Him and make Him known. However, there are standards for our vocation. Therefore, we as believers are to continually read and reference God's brand identity guide (the Bible). It is our reference point and a reminder of our instructions. 2 Corinthians 5:20 makes our role clear, *"We are therefore Christ's ambassadors, as though God were making his appeal through us. We implore you on Christ's behalf: Be reconciled to God."* Ensuring that His ambassadors understood how to properly represent his brand, God introduced a brand spokesperson – Jesus.

As we build and plant churches, it is not enough to just have a passion for the church, but we must also have a reverence and a respect for how God desires for His church to be represented. In doing this, we must be intentional about our **Brand Strategy**. It is also important that we look at Jesus for reference on how to build a brand.

The Jesus Brand Model

Jesus is the perfect example for mankind. He is the pinnacle of hope. In our daily lives, we as believers should aspire to become more like Him. Symbolically, Jesus is God's brand spokesperson. God sent His son to us to be the representation of His brand. The core message of the Bible, is a branding campaign for Jesus. It is only fitting that as we consider the necessity of branding ministry, we look to Jesus as the example. There are several instances recorded in the Bible, that display Jesus' brand model. In this section, we will look at a few of them.

Key Elements of the Jesus Brand Model:

<u>Define Your Brand Identity</u>

The first step in any branding process is defining who you are. It is nearly impossible to build a successful brand without having a clear definition of who you are, the values you hold and the benefit of what you offer. Before Jesus ever came to earth, his brand identity was being established. The prophet Isaiah gave us one of the earliest pronouncements of the Jesus Brand.

> *For unto us a Child is born, unto us a Son is given; and the government will be upon His shoulder. And His name will be called Wonderful, Counselor, Mighty God, Everlasting Father, Prince of Peace.*
>
> Isaiah 9:6 (NKJV)

Generations before Jesus was born, His brand campaign had already begun. Expectation and anticipation was already being established. The prelaunch to Jesus' brand began even before the prophet Isaiah, it started in Genesis chapter three. Long before His divine birth, the Jesus brand was being defined. Take a moment to consider how you would define your brand.

> **Long before His divine birth, the Jesus brand was being defined.**

Define Your Audience

Many organizations make the mistake of not conducting adequate research to understand the character and personalities of the specific people they intend to reach with their service. Particularly, without conducting the proper research and gaining adequate knowledge about the target audience, churches cannot experience lasting growth. Ministry exclusive of harvest targeted evangelism, will be ineffective. Every church should welcome people of any background and demographic, but there needs to be a deliberate strategy in place for reaching people. Some might argue that targeting specific people is not biblical, but audience targeting is very much so, a biblical strategy for reaching the world.

> **God's method and strategy for reaching the world was through a specific people.**

God has always desired to return all people back to Him. But His method for reaching everyone, often started by targeting a specific people. He has a targeted audience in His global strategy. God's plan for redemption started with Abram, then reached his family, his tribe and ultimately a nation to the world.

> *"As for Me, behold, My covenant is with you, and you shall be a father of many nations. No longer shall your name be called Abram, but your name shall be Abraham; for I have made you a father of many nations. I will make you exceedingly fruitful; and I will make nations of you, and kings shall come from you. And I will establish My covenant between Me and you and your descendants after you in their generations, for an everlasting covenant, to be God to you and your descendants after you. Also I give to you and your descendants after you the land in which you are a stranger, all the land of Canaan, as an everlasting possession; and I will be their God."*
>
> Genesis 17:4-8

God's method and strategy for reaching the world was through a specific people. Jesus also started with reaching a defined target audience. His audience was the Israelites. From among these people, He selected men to completely pour His wisdom and teaching into. Although His end goal was all people, the men He selected were not Greeks or Samaritans: they were Israelites. These men were Jesus' initial target audience for His brand. To grow any brand, you must start with a niche group and expand from those targeted people.

Define the Need Your Brand Meets

Every brand must define its benefits or the need that the brand was created to meet. The audience must be reminded that there is a problem and the brand solves the problem. Great brands create **utility**. They produce something more than what people want: they produce products that people need. Contemporary brands like Uber and Netflix were born as a solution to a perceived problem. Church branding must be clear about how fellowship with their congregation makes life better and is a solution to the needs of their audience. In the book of Luke, Jesus announces His brand's solution in a very audacious way.

> "And He was handed the book of the prophet Isaiah. And when He had opened the book, He found the place where it was written: "The Spirit of the Lord is upon, Me, Because He has anointed Me to preach the gospel to the poor; He has sent Me to heal the brokenhearted, to proclaim liberty to the captives and recovery of sight to the blind, to set at liberty those who are oppressed; to proclaim the acceptable year of the Lord." Then He closed the book, and gave it back to the attendant and sat down. And the eyes of all who were in the synagogue were fixed on Him. And He began to say to them, "Today this Scripture is fulfilled in your hearing."
>
> Luke 4:17-21

In this scripture, Jesus was very specific about the problems that His brand came to solve.

The Jesus Brand came to:
- *Preach good news to the poor*
- *Heal the brokenhearted*
- *Proclaim freedom to captives*
- *Give sight to the blind*
- *Free the oppressed*
- *Proclaim the year of the Lord (the favor of God)*

Although those in the synagogue were shocked, Jesus was very clear that the prophet Isaiah, gave an announcement of the brand that Jesus fulfilled. He could have kindly said to a few friends and family that He came to do all the things listed without saying that He was the fulfillment of Scripture. However, he wanted to grab their attention and He intended to be bold. After all, this was the announcement of His brand and He was confident that His brand could do all that was stated. Once again the Jesus model poses two imperative questions for you to ask yourself and answer honestly:

1. Are you explicitly aware of the problem(s) your brand intends to solve?
2. How confident are you in your brand's ability to solve those problems.

Conduct a Perception Check

In His three years of earthly ministry, Jesus was very specific and strategic about displaying and communicating the brand. His life and ministry displayed the brand model for building an effective church brand. The brand was important to Jesus and he consistently reinforced the principles of the brand to his first brand ambassadors – the disciples. In the sixteenth chapter of Matthew, we see Jesus conducting a perception check with His disciples.

Before He went to the cross, before He died and before He ascended to Heaven, Jesus conducted a perception check.

When Jesus came into the region of Caesarea Philippi, He asked His disciples, saying, "Who do men say that I, the Son of Man, am?" So they said, "Some say John the Baptist, some Elijah, and others Jeremiah or one of the prophets." He said to them, "But who do you say that I am?" Simon Peter answered and said, "You are the Christ, the Son of the living God." Jesus answered and said to him, "Blessed are you, Simon Bar-Jonah, for flesh and blood has not revealed this to you, but My Father who is in heaven. And I also say to you that you are Peter, and on this rock I will build My church, and the gates of Hades shall not prevail against it."

Matthew 16:13-18 (NKJV)

Before He went to the cross, before He died and before He ascended to Heaven, Jesus conducted a perception check. *"Who do men say that I, the Son of Man, am?"* Jesus understood that no matter how many miracles He did, His brand lived in the minds of His audience and would be communicated to others based on their mind's perceptions. While conducting a perception check, he ensured that His disciples knew that he was not John the Baptist, not Elijah or one of the prophets. Jesus confirmed that they perceived Him as the

Son of God. Jesus conducted **Brand Research**. How ironic that His first mention of "The Church" started after He identified His brand.

Jesus did not proceed without ensuring that the brand was properly communicated. His church could not be started without having a clear picture of who He was. The disciples were His first brand ambassadors. Before He could leave them, He had to be sure that His church was founded on the correct principles and that His ambassadors understood the brand. This is often in contrast of how many churches are started today. There is little thought placed into the foundation of the ministry and even less thought placed on communicating brand principles and standards to the individuals who represent the brand.

Select Your Brand Team

When launching a new brand, you need a team of people who believe in the brand and who are invested in the promotion of the brand. The people who support and believe in your brand are your brand ambassadors. They are the people who will tell their friends and family about your brand. They are the ones who attend planning meetings and ultimately, they are the people you trust to ensure the brand identity is properly represented. The brand ambassadors are the first point of contact with your consumers and should be completely trained in the vision of the brand, as well as its benefits.

Jesus was very intentional about educating and training the disciples as His brand ambassadors. He spent three years in training His team and demonstrating His brand. Endeavoring to ensure that when He was not around, they would represent His brand with the same care, passion and effectiveness. The Great Commission paints the picture of Jesus instructing His ambassadors (the disciples) to spread the news of and represent his brand. He also instructed them to make more ambassadors. The branding strategy of multiplying ambassadors is much like the process that has made the pyramid brands so successful. Their representatives are not only trained to market and represent the brand's products, but they are also trained on how to discover new talent and *convert* them into representatives.

> *Then the eleven disciples went away into Galilee, to the mountain which Jesus had appointed for them. When they saw Him, they worshiped Him; but some doubted. And Jesus came and spoke to them, saying, "All authority has been given to Me in heaven and on earth. Go therefore and make disciples of all the nations, baptizing them in the name of the Father and of the Son and of the Holy Spirit, teaching them to observe all things that I have commanded you; and lo, I am with you always, even to the end of the age." Amen.*
>
> Matthew 28:16-20(NKJV)

These first brand ambassadors must have done a pretty good job spreading the news of the brand and making more ambassadors. The Pew Research Center (pewforum.com) reported that there are 2.18 billion Christians of all ages around the world. This number represented a third of the global population. While there are plenty more people that need the proper exposure to Christianity, this represents great brand strategy and team selection. Consider your team, could they represent and carry on your brand for generations?

God is in the Detail

As the old saying goes, "God is in the details." Throughout Scripture we see God giving men precise strategy for battle and war, but we also see several instances where God was directly involved in the details such as the design of structures, temples and instruments of worship.

In the book of Genesis, we have an account of God instructing Noah on the specifications for the building of the Ark. God was very detailed in explaining the length, breadth and height of the large boat. God also gave Moses specific instructions for the construction of the tent or tabernacle where He would dwell. At the top of Mount Sinai, after a very detailed materials list, God gave Moses the precise pattern to use.

> *And let them make Me a sanctuary, that I may dwell among them. According to all that I show you, that is, the pattern of the tabernacle and the pattern of all its furnishings, just so you shall make it.*
>
> Exodus 25:8-9

In comparison, God created the world in six days, but used forty days to give Moses instructions on the tabernacle details. Even more detailed than the tabernacle are the instructions that God gave Moses for the design and construction of the Ark of Testimony. God was very specific about the type of wood and even the color of the fabrics used. There are several instances of God's involvement in the details, however, the most specific and detailed pattern for construction was the plans for the temple that David requested his son, Solomon, to build.

> *Then David gave his son Solomon the plans for the vestibule, its houses, its treasuries, its upper chambers, its inner chambers, and the place of the mercy seat; and the plans for all that he had by the Spirit, of the courts of the house of the Lord, of all the chambers all around, of the treasuries of the house of God, and of the treasuries for the dedicated things; also for the division of the priests and the Levites, for all the work of the service of the house of the Lord, and for all the articles of service in the house of the Lord.*
>
> 1 Chronicles 28:11-13

> *And David said to his son Solomon, "Be strong and of good courage, and do it; do not fear nor be dismayed, for the Lord God – my God – will be with you.*

He will not leave you nor forsake you, until you have finished all the work for
the service of the house of the Lord.

1 Chronicles 28:20

The pattern came from God. He was the architect and He designed His temple in a way that represented Him. The tabernacle and temple plans were so detailed because they testified and spoke of the character of God. He even selected the fabric and colors of the temple drapes. God is the master interior designer. The materials and craftsmanship displayed the excellency of God. As in brand design, the architecture, structure and drapery of the temple were created with unity and cohesiveness.

And he made fifty clasps of gold, and coupled the curtains to one another
with the clasps, that it might be one tabernacle.

Exodus 36:13

He also made fifty bronze clasps to couple the tent together, that it may be
one.

Exodus 36:18

In the Old Testament, these temples were God's dwelling places. In the life of Jesus, God dwelt in Him and among us. Now He dwells in us and symbolically in our churches. Both "temples" should be handled with care and consideration of the same level of detail God instructed concerning His dwelling places in Scripture. Our modern-day churches are God's dwelling places and are a representation of His brand. The process of building a church brand, including the selection of colors, designs, images and even names should be carefully planned and strategized because it is a representation of God.

Our modern-day churches are God's dwelling places and are a representation of His brand.

Effective branding requires the same level of attention to detail. Apple manages every detail of their branding, from the color schemes of their retail stores to the simplicity of their packaging. As with God and the design of the temple, everything is designed to be one or cohesive and consistent. Every time a person interacts with Apple, care and consideration for the details are displayed. Things that may seem minor or overlooked by the general eye, have gone through months and years of planning.

A common technique in business is **touch-point** analysis, which is a process of looking at every potential point of interaction a customer has with your brand. At each touch-point, you consider what is being communicated and if that message accurately reflects your brand. In a church, this can range from the logo, interior carpet selection to the website design. It all reflects your brand.

When starting your branding process, establish a clear understanding of what you want to communicate and identify even the smallest of details in each touch-point you have with your audience.

The Power of a Name

There is so much in a name. One of the first acts of authority that God gave Adam, was his ability to name a thing. Names were extremely important in Biblical settings. We frequently see God changing a person's name from one thing to another and revealing something new about their identity. One of the first examples of this is when God changed Abram's name (exalted father) to Abraham (father of a multitude). Even Jesus changed Simon's name to Cephas (which is translated Peter).

There are thousands of instances where the word "name" is referenced in Scripture. Names often represented a person's purpose and character. To name a person or a thing was not a responsibility that was taken lightly. It required thought and revelation from God. When appearing to a pregnant virgin named Mary, one of the first things the angel Gabriel said to her was the name she would give her child.

> The angel said to her, "Don't be afraid, Mary; God has shown you his grace. Listen! You will become pregnant and give birth to a son, and you will name him Jesus. He will be great and will be call the Son of the Most High. The Lord God will give him the throne of King David, his ancestor.
>
> Luke 1:30-32

Your church or organization's name is an extension of your brand. Names were not just haphazardly given. There was purpose and intent behind every name in the Bible. It is this same thought, direction and strategy that we should use when attempting to name our ministries and organizations. There is a certain power in a name. Not just spiritually, but even naturally. Your church or organization's name is an extension of your brand. It is important that you take time to ensure that your name means the things that you want your brand to represent. Names are so powerful that just hearing a brand's name could set the expectation in the mind of a potential member or believer of what will be received when encountering your brand.

It is also important that you select a name that is timeless and appeals to your target audience. A church with a dated, overly complicated or religious name could turn a prospective believer away before they can even make it to the door. I know it is tempting for churches to select names that sound powerful and "deep," but to an unbeliever, these names could be a little too dramatic to draw them in.

A name like "Emerging Church of the Sword and Spirit," sounds powerful and may appeal to a religious or "**churched**" person. Unfortunately, to the "unchurched," this name could be off-putting and intimidating. Selecting a ministry name that is only comprehended by church people means that you are only looking to attract currently churched people. This is the error that many churches make. They build their brands around things that appeal only to people who are currently churched, leaving the many unchurched individuals outside of our private church gatherings. What is even more confusing is when a name like the one above is coupled with a slogan like, "Reaching the Lost at any Cost." Overly religious names do not appeal to the lost and could not possibly be targeted to them.

Another thing that should be considered in the age of technology is selecting a name that can be translated well as a website **URL**. Names that are too long or complicated to spell will have a hard time becoming highly visited websites. When selecting a URL name, it should be your brand name and if not, should be easily referenced to your brand name. It should also be short and not include numbers or hyphens. (I will explain more about URL names and websites in chapter seven.)

The perfect brand name should be timeless, easy to say and easy to remember. The perfect brand name should be timeless, easy to say and easy to remember. The brand name should also stand for something that communicates your core values and allows room for brand extensions. When choosing a name brands should consider if it will look good in an email, text and in a logo. A brand name is one of an organizations most valuable assets. Choosing the wrong name can hinder all communication efforts.

There must a be strategy when selecting a great brand name. This name tells people who you are and ideally will be with you for a long time. If you are starting a new ministry or rebranding a current ministry, use the steps below to help develop your brand name strategy.

The Brand Name Selection Process:

Step 1 - *Define the Audience and Goals*

In this step, you are to take time and define who you are trying to reach and what you want the name to achieve. The brand name should appeal to the audience that you are trying to reach. It should not confuse them or take an explanation to get them to understand why you chose the name or what it means. This is also the time where you should consider what you want the name to achieve. Consider if you want a name that welcomes people or a name that shocks them. Either option can be effective, but you need to consider the one that best reflects your goals.

Step 2 - *Consider the Adjectives and Feelings*

In this step, you should consider the adjectives and feelings that you previously drafted in Chapter 1, to describe your brand's association. The name that you select should reflect those same sentiments and should not be contradictory. If you selected an adjective like "Fresh" and an emotion like "Rejuvenated," a name like "Battle Axe Church of Fire," would not be a great example of those nouns. The name you choose should reflect those word choices.

Step 3 - *Generate a list of Potential Names*

At this point, begin to draft a list of potential names for your brand. I would recommend at least five different names that have gone through the previous two steps. Once you have created your list, evaluate your potential names against the criteria listed below.

Criteria for a good brand name:
- It must sound great when spoken.
- It won't be easily mispronounced or misspelled.
- It relates to your target audience.
- It works well as a URL.
- It is not in use by any other church or similar organization.
  Trademark infringement can be very expensive to your organization. Before you select a name, you can use the U.S. Patent and Trademark Office's (*www.uspto.gov*) trademark search tool, to see if the name or variations of it are currently in use.

After you have taken the name through these processes, select the name that best represents your brand.

Step 4 - *Protect Your Brand Name*

The final, but most important step is to protect your brand name. Once you have selected a brand name, you are ready to apply for trademark protection. A trademark legal protects words, names, symbols and logos that distinguish your brand. Your brand name is one of your most valuable assets and should be protected. Completing this step prevents other groups or organizations from using your name or associating themselves with your brand. For a step by step process for applying for trademark protection, visit www.uspto.gov. Please beware, there are several companies that advertise assistance with applying for trademark protection. However, not all of these companies are legitimate and due diligence should be done before paying for any service.

Now that you have a great name that accurately reflects your brand and is fully protected, you are ready to immerse yourself into a comprehensive branding process.

Activity 2

Generate Names

Take a moment to draft a list of potential names for your brand. Use the adjectives and feelings from Activity 1 to aid you in your name generation.

Try to assess the quality of your brand names with the following questions.

- *Does it sound great when said aloud?*
- *Is it easily pronounced and spelled by others?*
- *Does it match your target Audience?*
- *Will it work as a URL?*
- *Is it in use by another organization?*

"If people believe they share values with a company, they will stay loyal to the brand."

– Howard Schultz, CEO of Starbucks

3

Deploying the Branding Process

Now that we have established a basis for the need of branding a church or ministry organization, we can move towards the application of practical branding strategy. There are a few components to deploying and executing an effective branding process that we will explore. These strategies require clear thought and focus.

> **It is impossible to get someone to buy into or become more interested in something that you cannot clearly define or explain.**

It is impossible to get someone to buy into or become more interested in something that you cannot clearly define or explain. You should be able to quickly and easily explain why your church or organization is so great and provide detail about what makes it different. In business, this is called the elevator pitch. This simple exercise is a snapshot of your brand's product or service, summarized in 30 seconds or less, the time it would take you to explain something to someone else on an elevator ride.

Keep in mind, an elevator pitch is not about how fast you talk, it's about how well you know your product or service. You should be about to communicate your brand in an authentic and memorable way, at a moment's notice. If someone asked you, *"What makes your church great?"* or *"Why is your music so great?"* would you be able to articulate your answer effectively in 30 seconds or less?

In this chapter, we will explore the definition, differential makeup, and specific audience of your brand.

Knowing the Product or Service

Effective brand strategy will result in honest reflection on who your church or organization is and what you offer to people. No proper branding strategy or campaign can start without having a clear understanding of the product or service that you intend to brand. Understanding the brand's product or service goes beyond your brand simply being "a church" or "a school" or "a fitness center." You must take ask yourself, *"How does this church or organization make the lives of people better?"* What do you offer to enhance the lives of your brand audience? Regardless of the nature of your organization, you must have a clear vision of your brand's product or service offerings. This means identifying the qualities and characteristics of your brand. Branding thrives when there is a cohesive awareness of who you are as a church, business or organization.

Your brand definition is a declaration of what your brand stands for.	The first step in knowing your product or service is to define your brand. To do this, you may use the list of adjectives that you developed in Chapter 1, to assist you attempt to define your brand. Your **Brand Definition** is a declaration of what your brand stands for. It is different from a vision or mission statement that we will discuss in the next chapter. The brand definition details what you are offering and why you are offering it.

It is the benefits that are received when encountering your brand. This becomes your product or service.

For example, at All Nations Worship Assembly we use the phrase "Be Healed, Be Delivered and Be Set Free." This phrase is printed on shirts, banners and brochures. It is different from our slogan, it is our brand definition. It could also be considered as our brand tagline. This memorable phrase tells people our brand promise. People know that when they encounter our brand, they will be healed, delivered and set free. Ultimately, we are a church that is branding healing, deliverance and freedom. Now, before you scoff at the idea of branding these human needs, remember Jesus' declaration in Luke 4. This proclamation was Jesus' brand definition. He identified the benefit of his brand.

Every organization must define and know their product or service prior to developing or communicating their brand. Without having a clear picture of the product or service, none of your branding (logos, slogans, advertising, customer service, etc.) will display a cohesive message. Messages that are not cohesive will lack credibility. When defining your brand, make sure you use things that your ministry or organization currently does and not things that you wish or aspire to do.

Healthy families, freedom, purpose and education are all examples of great ministry brand services. While every ministry or church should offer these benefits, there should be certain things that are the primary focus of your ministry. The brand definition should focus on the things that the ministry does best. This is a great time to consider the things that your ministry does best. Take a minute to consider your ministry or organization's strengths. Awareness of these strengths will help you to determine your Brand Audience.

Defining the Brand Audience

Once you have a clear picture of what you intend to brand, you are now ready to consider your brand audience. Your Brand Audience also known as a **Target Audience**, is the specific group of people that you intend to reach with your branding efforts. As I discussed in chapter two, even Jesus had a target audience. Every brand must have a specific group that they desire to reach, with their brand message.

Traditionally, defining a brand audience has been considered a best business practice. However, establishing a defined empathy with the audience that you intend to serve is also a wise strategy for a church and any other organization. Having a description of your brand audience, you will have a

55

basis for making decisions like offering programs, services, and even selecting the stage design and interior décor for your church. Having a defined audience will also help you to make strategic decisions about who to communicate with and how to communicate with them.

One of the biggest mistakes that churches and new start up organizations make is trying to appeal to everyone. This cookie cutter and undifferentiated approach to communicating is not effective. Great brands focus on a specific audience and design a brand that people will want to be a part of. Even Paul taught that to reach an audience, you must specifically appeal to that audience.

> *For though I am free from all men, I have made myself a servant to all, that I might win the more; and to the Jews I became as a Jew, that I might win Jews; to those who are under the law, as under the law, that I might win those who are under the law; to those who are without law, as without law (not being without law toward God, but under law toward Christ), that I might win those who are without law; to the weak I became as weak, that I might win the weak. I have become all things to all men, that I might by all means save some.*
>
> 1 Corinthians 9:19-22

Knowing the specific group of people that you want to reach is an important part of the branding process and should not be overlooked. Below are the steps for defining your brand audience:

Step One: Define the Demographics

Demographics refers to the statistical data and characteristics of a selected population. The most common branding and marketing demographics include:

- **Age** - *The average age of your audience.*
- **Gender** – *The primary gender of your audience*
- **Nationality** – *The primary nationality, ethnicity and language of your audience*
- **Geographic Location** – *The primary geographic location of your audience*

- **Household Composition** – *The marital status and average number of children in the household*
- **Education Level** – *The average highest education level of your audience*
- **Career Status** – The primary employment status of your audience
- **Income Level** – The average income range of your audience

The more refined this list is, the easier it will be to implement your brand strategy. If you know the primary age, gender and education of your audience, you can design your brand and your brand strategy in a way that appeals to that group of people. If you are launching a new brand, you can conduct a study of the people in the community where you intend to launch your brand. The United States Census Bureau website (census.gov) provides a helpful tool called American FactFinder, which provides demographic information by region, state, city and zip code. Great brands opt for creating meaningful and lasting experiences for a specific group of people, as opposed to trying to please all people. Defining the demographics of your audience will help you brand your organization in a way that appeals most to them.

Step Two: Define the Behavioral Patterns

Behavioral patterns refer to the needs, wants, desires and motivations of your brand audience. The most common branding and marketing behavioral patterns include:
- **Interests** – *The spare-time activities and hobbies of your audience*
- **Information Sources** – *The information sources that your audience uses (Websites, Radio Stations, Magazines, Television Programs, Social Media Sites, etc.)*
- **Beliefs** – *The social, political and religious convictions that your audience holds*

When you have a description that includes the demographics and the behavioral patterns of the people you are trying to reach, you equip yourself with the information you need to address their needs, wants, desires and motivations. Defining your brand audience helps you better serve the people you desire to impact and gives you direction on how to reach them to evoke your desired response. Brands that truly excel deliver benefits that customers truly desire. You don't just start a church or a business simply because you want to, but you start them because you desire to fulfill the needs of a people. A brand must know both the people and their needs in order to truly excel.

> People will do the things that you desire, if the actions and processes to do them are made very simple.

Determining the Desired Response

Every action and every reach that God makes in a person's life has an intended purpose and a desired response from the affected person. Ultimately, God desires for men to turn from the lusts of the flesh and return to Him. He plans, He strategizes and He reaches with intention. God's branding efforts all have a desired response or outreach.

Before you can successfully execute your brand strategy, it is important to have a clear idea of the response that you desire for your audience to make. There should be a goal for every branding activity. Successful organizations start building brands with an idea for a desired audience response from the start of their planning process. For example; a coffee company may brand their coffee to be a morning necessity. Their slogans, commercials and images will all reflect that a cup of their coffee is the best part of the morning. The goal of this strategy is to get their brand audience to buy their coffee and start every morning with a cup of it.

Similarly, a church or ministry should also have a clear picture of the response that they desire their audience to make. While there may be a series of small decisions; like viewing services online visiting the church, ultimately, the desired response for any church should be to inspire a person to walk the aisle and join the church. In the end, the desired outcome depends on the goals you set from the start of your branding strategy.

One thing to remember is that no matter what your desired response or outcome is, people respond to branding strategies based on simple details that may be overlooked if not properly strategized. People will do the things that you desire, if the actions and processes to do them are made very simple. Anything that is too complicated for people to do or understand, they will not do. Remove the complexities and your response rate will be higher. When planning our churches and services, make sure that it is easy for people to get to the desired outcome.

Let's take for example, the process of paying for services or goods with credit cards. These simple, plastic cards have virtually replaced checks and are close to replacing cash. Most businesses offer credit card processing for purchases because they make it easy for people to spend more money, even when they didn't plan on it. You can walk into a store, with a friend, without the intent of buying anything for yourself. While in that store, if you see something that you like, you don't have to wait until you come back with cash. You can just pull out your card and make the purchase on the spot. This is the desired response of almost any business.

With this simplicity and convenience in mind, the church must make it easy for people to not only attend a service, but they must also make it easy for people to engage with the ministry and in the end, engage with God. Some things to keep in mind when thinking of your desired responses or outcomes include:

- If you want people to visit your website, make sure that the URL is not too complicated to remember.
- If you want people to attend your church, make sure that the church address is easily located and visible on your church website.
- If you want parents to enjoy the service, make sure that you offer child care to prevent them from being distracted by a restless child during the service.
- If you want people to join your church, make sure that the process of joining is not too complicated.

- Even the call to salvation must be clear, direct and simple.

No matter what your desired response may be, make sure that a major part of your strategy is making it as simple as possible for people to act. It doesn't matter that you have a great brand and a great ministry, if your brand doesn't achieve the desired response. If the process for interaction is complicated or poor, the audience's response will change.

The chart below illustrates some goals to consider when attempting to get people to your desired response.

Chart 3.1 **Response Driven Goals**

Goals	Explanation
Revelation	Does your audience know who you are?
Attention	Does your brand grab the attention of your audience?
Grasp	Is your brand too complicated for your audience to understand the benefits?
Convincing	Does your brand offer claims that lack believability?
Interest	Does your brand lack an immediate perceived need?

Having a branding strategy that is simple, interesting and applicable to your brand audience has the most probability of achieving the desired response. Take a moment to consider the response or outcome that you desire from your brand audience. Once complete, you will have the framework for strategic and effective branding.

Setting the Brand Apart

Another key component to building an effective brand, is having a clear understanding of what sets your brand apart from the competition. Now of course, it may seem odd to consider a church as having competition, but the fact remains, competition is out there. The first thought is to think of churches as competing with other churches, and while that may partially be true, there is a greater competition. Consumerism. We live in a highly media saturated society. Churches primarily compete with other churches for members and new believers, but they compete with the human desire for self-fulfillment, offered by marketplace goods and services. Companies are constantly upgrading and improving how they present their product offerings to give consumers the feeling that they are pursuing something new.

> To thrive, churches must compete with consumer products that claim to offer identity and meaning.

To thrive, churches must compete with consumer products that claim to offer identity and meaning. As much as we wish and hope that this was not the case, the reality is that it is true. The church must learn how to "out-reach" the marketplace. While the consumerist products and services only offer false solutions for identity and meaning, their options are plentiful. There are so many options available that a person could go a lifetime trying other services without ever looking to the church for the solution. Not to mention the fact that many churches do not do a good job at representing the Kingdom.

Additionally, we live in a time where religious worship does not have to be linked to a time or location. Individuals can worship at any time of day and without even leaving the comfort of their homes. With solutions as simple as a YouTube search or purchasing a book from a local retailer, people can worship God without ever entering a brick and mortar church building. This convenience has added additional competition for churches who seek to draw people into a building for "assembling together," as the Bible instructs us in the book of Hebrews. To remain relevant, the

Church must have an awareness of the things that compete for the attention of the potential new believer. They must motivate people to gather together in worship.

Another point to consider is that not every type of church will appeal to every person. This is not a bad thing. We live in a world full of people with various backgrounds, histories and nationalities. God created us as unique races and unique individuals. It would be detrimental for us to assume that every church should be "One-Size-Fits-All." It is helpful to illustrate and point out the character of a church. Or as I like to call it, the "DNA." Every church and every organization has a personality and character or "DNA." The components of Ministry, Branding and Culture make up a churches DNA.

Illustration 3.1 Church DNA

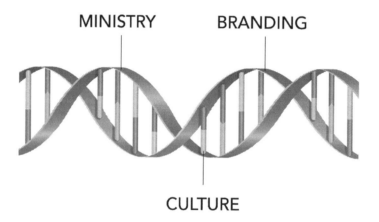

MINISTRY   BRANDING

CULTURE

God is the master Creator, therefore we should be able to point out unique attributes in our churches and organizations that God designed to differentiate us. Successful brands are cognizant of these core values and they highlight them. They provide the unchurched with the awareness that not only is church important for everyone, but that there is a church for everyone. You must also be aware of what makes you different from other organizations in your category.

It is also important to be different because the human cognitive system acts a as a filter to protect our minds from large amounts of irrelevant and unnecessary information. Our brains learn to respond to things that stand out. It is a protective mechanism that prevents us from entering into to danger. The same filter that helps us avoid thinking a cat and a tiger are the same, works to differentiate products and services. Brands must identify the distinguishing features that set them apart from the competition.

> Our brains learn to respond to things that stand out.

The distinguishing features of a brand are what is commonly referred to in the business world as the Unique Selling Proposition (USP). Your USP is the distinctive core elements that make you stand out from the rest.

To develop your USP, consider the questions below:
- Is your brand unique?
- How is your brand unique?
- Can it be proven?
- If you are not unique, how do you do what you do better than the competition?

To truthfully answer these questions, this step requires thoughtful research of any potential competition.

Research into the competition, whether it is marketplace goods or services, other religions or other churches; should include answering some or all of the questions listed below:

- Who is the competition?
- What are their values?
- Who is their target audience?
- What are their weaknesses?

- What are their strengths?
- How do they look and feel?

It is also important to understand that it is not enough to just be different. Great brands always demonstrate their difference, to make it easy for their audience to understand that difference. Successful differentiation is communicated through brand story telling.

Telling the Story: Communicate

The Bible is a great continuous story about the fall of man and his redemption through Jesus, told through several smaller stories. There are 52 pivotal stories that make up this redemption story, 26 in the Old Testament (before the birth of Jesus) and 26 in the New Testament (during the life of Jesus and beyond). At the heart of Christianity's success has been the human ability to communicate through the art of storytelling. The Old Testament itself exists because of generations of God inspired story telling. This same type of communication is what helps to build successful brands.

With strategic brand storytelling, churches can build brands that last.

For years, pastors have mastered the art of storytelling. The 52 pivotal Bible stories have been successfully told by church leaders in different formats, and with varied emphasis and expression for centuries. However, the story of the church and the importance of ministry has been communicated with lackluster effectiveness. The church can express the story of the Nativity with detail, but falters when it comes to conveying the importance and the relevance of the church in a way that inspires people to commune. With strategic brand storytelling, churches can build brands that last.

Don't get me wrong, I am not speaking of the "once upon a time," or the fanciful make-believe type of stories. I am referencing the honest and truthful stories that are told through tools like a PowerPoint presentation, a brochure or a well-designed website; paired with people who believe in the integrity and authenticity of the story. To reach new believers, churches must tell brand stories that are authentic, consistent and inspiring.

Your brand reflects your core values and beliefs, it should communicate the story of what you stand for across every area. High end car brands tell their stories of luxury and success in every touch point from the website to their in-store sales floors. The customer is constantly reminded the brand represents another level of living. Likewise, churches must communicate the principles of their story in their interactions with potential members. A true brand story will speak for your church or organization and can be recalled when your audience begins to doubt your brand or consider the competition.

A great biblical example of this is John the Baptist's question from prison and Jesus' response to it. Jesus' year of popularity was beginning to change to a time of opposition. John the Baptist was imprisoned and appeared to be experiencing some doubt about Jesus' brand.

> *When Jesus finished placing this charge before his twelve disciples, he went on to teach and preach in their villages. John, meanwhile, had been locked up in prison. When he got wind of what Jesus was doing, he sent his own disciples to ask, "Are you the One we've been expecting, or are we still waiting?" Jesus told them, "Go back and tell John what's going on: The blind see, the lame walk, lepers are cleansed, the deaf hear, the dead are raised, the wretched of the earth learn that God is on their side. "Is this what you were expecting? Then count yourselves most blessed!"*
>
> Matthew 11:1-6 (MSG)

Essentially, Jesus reminded them of His actions or as the retail world calls it, His "Product Demonstration." A product demonstration is an exhibition of a products abilities to potential customers. The work that Jesus did demonstrated His abilities, told His story and communicated the principles of his brand. His actions matched His brand promise. The brand promise and actions of a church must communicate a cohesive story. Effective communication of this story is what will make visitors become members and those members will become brand ambassadors.

Activity 3 *Competitive* *Review*	Take a moment to draft a list of potential competitors to your brand. The answer the questions below for each potential competitor. • Who is the competition? • What are their values? • Who is their target audience? • What are their weaknesses? • What are their strengths? • How do they look and feel?

"If people can't see what God is doing, they stumble all over themselves; But when they attend to what he reveals, they are most blessed."

– Proverbs 29:18 (MSG)

4

Establishing a Brand Mission and Vision

The brand vision and mission has been the center piece of business organizations for many years. The mission and vision drive the brand strategy and filters decisions that are made throughout the organization. Both serve individual functions, but are often confused. When planning and strategizing, it is important to understand their differences and purposes. While the mission of the Church as a whole should be to do the things that Jesus and the Apostles commanded it to do, individual churches should define their individual approach to becoming an effective piece to a larger body. Equally as important, is the vision statement of the church. Vision is one of the most overused words in the church world however, not many churches apply strategy to vision casting. As a distinct member of the Church, local churches should plan and forecast for the future. The church mission is always in service to the vision. The way that I define it is, your mission is the HOW and your vision is the WHY. Or another way to put it, your mission is the NOW, while your vision is the FUTURE.

The mission and vision, not the events, ministries and activities are what should drive a church.

The conversation about understanding purpose has been a topic of discussion in the church, but few churches put the adequate amount of effort into really defining their mission and vision. A church should have a clear understanding of the reason it exists and it should be known by anyone that is connected to the ministry. The mission and vision, not the events, ministries and activities are what should drive a church.

In this chapter, I will breakdown the reasons why a church needs to a have vision and mission statement. I will also define their distinct differences. By the end of this chapter, you will also learn some best practices for communicating these statements internally and externally.

Why Should a Church Have Vision and Mission Statements?

Vision and Mission statements are not just great tools for business. One of the greatest resources that God gives to church leaders that He has called, is the ability to cast vision. Vision is a glimpse into the future of the church. A church without a vision is a church on the fast track to nowhere. You can't create vision without first having a purpose. You must dream, receive revelation and direction from God. Many churches fail to come up with a vision and mission statement because they haven't put much thought into where they are going, or because they don't know how to start the process. However, developing the vision and mission statements is just as important as selecting the right building or location. For a church, these tools help the church organize and fulfill what God has called it to do. They also give church leaders and members a common goal to aspire towards. Habakkuk 2:2 explains this very clearly.

> And then God answered: "Write this. Write what you see. Write it out in big block letters so that it can be read on the run. This vision-message is a witness pointing to what's coming. It aches for the coming – it can hardly wait! And it doesn't lie. If it seems slow in coming, wait. It's on its way. It will come right on time.
>
> Habakkuk 2:2-3 (MSG)

Your brand should align with your vision and mission, as it reflects what your church stands for. The vision and mission statements communicate your organizations values and purpose. The absence of, or poorly written, church vision and mission statements are lost opportunities for attracting and engaging new believers and members. It also hinders a church's ability to build organizational "DNA" or culture. The vision and mission statements will also serve as the glue that holds things in your church together, as leaders may change, but a clearly defined vision and mission will encourage your people to focus on the "big picture." A good vision will build the faith of the people. The vision and mission statements should not exist as an abstract idea to the people.

As you embark on your branding strategy, the vision and mission statements will guide the development of your brand image and your reach for people.

The Difference Between a Vision and a Mission

Most churches tend to combine the vision and mission statements. The two are related but each has a very different objective. While they are commonly used interchangeably, it is important to have both. One doesn't work without the other, the vison statement gives purpose to the directives of the mission statement. Having purpose and definition are imperative for any church or organization, thus church leaders should not only understand the purpose of the two statements but should also make the effort to understand their differences.

The Vision Statement

The vision statement is about seeing. Its goal is to inspire the reader to believe in your organizations purpose. The vison statement is future focused and should be a big picture view of your ministry aspirations. It should illustrate what your church holds as its core principles and what it endeavors to become. When considering a vision statement, ask yourself this question: *If this church were to achieve our goals, what would it look like in 10-20 years?* Successful brands are driven by leaders who can inspire others to see a bigger and brighter future.

The Mission Statement

The mission statement is about doing. Its goal is to inform the reader of how you will achieve your purpose. While the vision is about the future, the mission is about what is currently done or needs to be done in order to get to the desired future. The mission is short-term and attainable. It should focus the efforts of your church on unified goals for making the vision a reality. Think of it as the road that leads to your vision. The mission statement may also change as you get closer to the vision and your methods of accomplishment change.

How to Define a Vision Statement

If you think small, your church will be small. Think big. A vision statement is not specific small goals or strategies such as "Building a 4,000-seat worship facility", or "Opening a community center for youth." The vision statement is how God sees your church. It is the reason that your church exists. If you think small, your church will be small. The vison should be more than just a statement. It should be a description of what your church will look like in the future. This statement must paint a picture of the future that will be revealed as you carry out your mission. This statement will give direction to every activity and decision made in your church. I love the way Proverbs 29 speaks about a people who can't see the vision.

> *If people can't see what God is doing, they stumble all over themselves; But when they attend to what he reveals, they are most blessed.*
>
> Proverbs 29:18

The best way to define your vision statement is to have a Vision Session with key persons in your ministry. A vison session is a meeting with a group of stakeholders that involves asking the group to appraise the current state of the organization and where they realistically expect to be in the future. I would even recommend that you invite an objective person to be a part of this meeting as well. You need someone that is not connected with the ministry who can offer an outside opinion. When you gather for the session, have a whiteboard or a large tablet to write out ideas and to spark creativity.

Together, your group should answer the following questions:
- How and where do we see ourselves in the future?
- What impact do we desire to make in the world?
- Who and what are we inspiring to change?
- What values are important to us?

Use the various answers to select the most important choices. Use these answers to develop your vision statement. Avoid using unnecessary words, in an attempt to make your vision sound more dramatic. There is nothing more wasteful than a vision statement full of words that lack immediate comprehension. Your church members, volunteers and staff should be able to recall and repeat your vision at any given time. Your vision statement should be purpose driven and should help to focus your team on why they show up and serve each week. It should also be innovative and promote growth.

Chart 4.1 **Keys to an Effective Vision Statement**

Keys	Explanation
Futuristic	The vision statement should speak to where the organization is going.
Meaningful	The vision statement should stand for something and should have a defined set of values.
Authentic	The vision statement should be genuine and reflect who the organization is actively aspiring to become.
Different	The vision statement should display the principles that make the organization distinct.

How to Define a Mission Statement

Your mission statement should define how you will reach your vision. It should be short and direct. The things listed in your mission statement should be action oriented and achievable. Just as you did when developing the vision statement, gather your team to create the mission statement.

In the process of defining a mission statement, a church should ask the following questions:

- *What do we do?*
- *Why do we do it?*
- *Whom do we serve?*
- *How do we serve them?*
- *How are we unique?*

If your mission statement does not compel actions toward the vision, then you do not have a good mission statement. It is essential that your mission statement connects with the heart of the people that you lead. The mission should be one that people will desire to achieve. It is what visitors and members will identify with. The mission statement should reach out and grab your audience and compel them towards forward movement.

> **The mission should be one that people will desire to achieve.**

Once you have finalized your mission statement, it should be reviewed every three to five years for measuring achievement and for adjusting or adding new missions. The chart below details some keys to a good mission statement.

Chart 4.2 Keys to a Good Mission Statement

Keys	Explanation
Clear	The mission statement should be written with such simplicity that it is easy to understand.
Memorable	The mission statement should be one that is easy to recite and remember.
Convicting	The mission statement should be worded in a way that inspires specific and realistic actions towards the vision.
Measurable	The mission statement should be something that can be measured for achievement year after year.
Concise	The mission statement should be no more than 15-18 words long, If it does go longer, it should be broken down into clear bullet points.

Communicating the Vision and Mission

Once the vision and mission statements have been finalized, it is time to think through a communication plan to share them with the members, volunteers and employees. One of the biggest elements of your communication plan is to make sure that the vision and mission statements are visible to the entire team. As Habakkuk said, it needs to be visible to everyone, as a motivation tool for those who serve. The people need to see how they individually fit into the vision and mission of your church or organization.

The future of your church must be shared consistently with the people that you lead. Think of several areas and ways to communicate the vision and mission into everything that you do. Your activities and functions shouldn't drive your vision and mission, it should be the other way around. The vision and mission should drive everything that you do. You will never see your vision become a reality until you have successfully communicated it with your target audience.

Below are ways of communicating the vision and mission statements:

New Members Class

The New Members Class is the first point of contact with new believers and/or members. The vision and mission statements should be a major teaching point for this class. Members should be reminded why these things are important to the ministry and should be shown how the mission and vision are incorporated into the functions of the ministry. They should also be encouraged to memorize them.

Pulpit Teaching

The pulpit has the most significant influence over anything else in the church. Including the vision and mission in the Sunday teaching and sermons is one of the best ways to communicate them to the church. The pastor should always be casting vision and informing the church on how to get there. Communicating the vision is an ongoing responsibility of the senior pastor and the leaders.

Leadership Development

As Senior Pastors plan the development of new elders, associate pastors and other leaders, the inclusion of the vision and mission into their training materials is a great way to communicate vision from the top down. Once the highest level of leaders have vision buy-in, they are more likely to communicate that vision to those who serve under them.

Decision Making

When decisions about activities, events and even large purchases are being made, training your team to consistently ask the question "How does this decision support the vision?" is an effective way to ingrain and communicate the vison to your people.

Interior Display

Displaying your vision inside your church is a simple way to constantly remind people of your church's vision and mission. Some churches have found success by hanging posters or banners within your church's hallways or entry ways. Another more modern way is to dedicate an entire interior wall to posting large letter decals that display the vision.

Website

A churches website has the greatest reach. If displayed on the website, not only will members have access to the mission and vision, but visitors will also be able to view these statements. They also should be easy to locate without having to conduct a major website search to find. Two of the most popular locations are the "Home" page and the "About Us" page of the website.

Print Materials

Print Materials are another way to visually communicate your vision and mission. Many churches use church brochures and bulletins to highlight their statements. You can also include them in your training materials for Sunday school and Christian education classes.

People

Your people are your greatest means for communicating your vision and mission statements. When they have bought into the vision, they communicate it in everything that they do. It is important to consistently remind the staff, leaders and volunteers of why the ministry exists and who it exists to serve.

The list above is not the only options for communicating your vision and mission statements. Depending on the nature of your church or organization, there may be several other ways to communicate with them. This list simply serves as a launching pad. Once complete, the vision and mission statements will become the steering wheel to drive the development of your brand identity.

They will also drive the alignment of all of your actions and activities. When you have perfectly aligned your actions and activities to the vision and mission, a stranger can walk into your church and infer your values based on your operations of your church. The process of alignment may be one of your most important strategies.

Remember that the mission and vision must be maintained. So, audit them frequently. If your church or organization is already in operation and you have just defined or refined your mission and vision statements, feel free to change or adjust anything that doesn't fit. Then going forward, let every decision be weighed by the principles of these statements.

Activity 4

Select a group for your Vision Session

Draft a list of people who would be helpful in participating in your Vision Session. Once you have a list of names, schedule a date for the session. Remember to use the questions below as the launching pad for your statements.

Vision Statement Questions:
- How and where do we see ourselves in the future?
- What impact do we desire to make in the world?
- Who and what are we inspiring to change?
- What values are important to us?

Mission Statement Questions:
- What do we do?
- Whom do we serve?
- How do we serve them?
- How are we unique?

"I'm here to build something for the long-term. Anything else is a distraction."

– Mark Zuckerberg, Founder of Facebook

5

Designing a Brand Identity

Now that you know who you are, who you are trying to reach and where you are going, you are now ready to design your brand identity. Your brand identity is the face of your brand. Brand identity includes your logo, name, color choices, pictures, videos and taglines. All visual elements associated with your brand make up your brand identity. The identity of any brand should be driven by the vision and mission statements, which should be timeless.

The use of logos, colors, type, pictures and video construct your brand identity. After establishing the elements of your brand's identity, apply them consistently across all communication efforts.

It is believed that humans make an average of 35,000 decisions each day. Branding elements help individuals in their decisions to either trust your church or business over an alternative. The elements of colors, typography, pictures and video all help to build a recognizable and effective brand. These elements will establish validity and longevity for your brand. Churches and organizations should meticulously plan how they will implement each element to build a cohesive brand story.

Churches must be deliberate in establishing their brand identity.

A clear understanding of how each visual element affects a person's response to your brand will help you build an effective brand identity. Churches must be deliberate in establishing their brand identity. In this chapter, I will help to define brand identity and detail the key elements in its makeup.

What is Brand Identity

Brand Identity is the method of visually communicating the values of your brand. If you think of your brands language as verbal communication (What you say) then consider your brand identity as visual communication (How you say it). Brand Identity is your brand's body language. Effective branding cannot exist without thoughtful strategy for how you present your brand visually. Churches and organizations that desire a brand strategy that produces, must develop brand identity guidelines. Brand identity guidelines are the parameters for how a brand will communicate. They express the look and feel of an organization.

These guidelines should contain guidance for the visual elements listed below.

Chart 5.1 **Elements for Brand Identity Guidelines**

Keys	Explanation
Logos	Easily recognizable symbols or graphics that represents your brand.
Design Elements	Patterns and shapes that are used in materials such as merchandise packaging, presentations and fabrics.
Colors	The selection of specific core colors that are used to identify the brand and create an emotion.
Typography/Fonts	Selecting specific typeface (fonts) to complement your color scheme and design themes.
Photography	The use of specific photographic images to tell your brand story.
Videos	The use of video in the form of ad, livestreams and other platforms to tell your brand story.

Using Logos that Support

Designing an effective logo or brand mark is a combination of blending art and vision. It should stand out and authentically represent the church or organization's values and unique offering. A logo is an easily recognizable graphic symbol or design that represents an organization and its products or services.

When creating a logo for your organization, the process should be focused on making a graphic image that is immediately recognizable, instils trust and admiration. It should also be a combination of shapes and colors that are apparently different from any other organization and that represent the brand values. Logos are a major part of brand identity. They require thought, creativity and good design to be great.

When selecting a designer to create your logo, first review their previous work. Look for designers whose work stands out to you most. A logo is a major asset and should be a lasting brand representation, so choose wisely. I also recommend that when signing a logo design agreement, clients should make sure that they are provided with at least six options to choose from, with a minimum of three revisions to whichever design is selected. This gives you some flexibility without requiring you to have to pay out more money for minor adjustments.

Additionally, you should consider all the ways that you may want to use your logo. It needs to look good as well as be identifiable and legible in its smallest form, to its largest form. The quality of the logo should be maintained if it is on a ballpoint pen or a large outdoor sign. All too often, organizations select logos that look good on a computer or a sheet of paper, but never consider how it will look as an app icon or another small form.

To effectively select or design an effective logo, it is important for you to understand the different types of logo elements.

Pictorial Mark

Pictorial Marks can be symbols or shapes that represent a brand. Its shape can be a literal or symbolic representation of the brand and its services. This graphic should be able to stand alone and still represent the brand.

Illustration 5.1 **Pictorial Mark**

Wordmark

The wordmark is usually the brand's name written or in acronym form, using a specific and identifiable font. The distinctive characteristics of the font or the structure of the font should be unique enough, to stand alone and be identifiable as the brand.

Illustration 5.2 **Wordmark**

Rockhills

CHRISTIAN CENTER

Letterform Mark

A letterform mark traditionally uses the first letter of the brand name and embellishes it enough to make it distinctive and identifiable. The single letter itself, becomes the focal point of the design.

Illustration 5.3 **Letterform Mark**

Brand Signature

The brand signature is the combination of all logo elements juxtaposed with the wordmark and tagline. See the example below. The need for each of these elements depends on the organization. The signature should be consistent and nonnegotiable.

Illustration 5.4 **Brand Signature**

Using Colors that Express

It is important to have a clear understanding of the biblical uses of color, it will help to validate why color usage has to be purposeful and strategic. The first thing that God created was light. This light was both visible and spiritual, but for the context of this topic, we will only review the visible aspects of the light. To see color, you have to first have light. Most light sources, such as the sun contain all colors mixed together, which produces white light. When that light shines on objects, some colors bounce off the objects and others are absorbed by the objects. The human eye only sees the colors that are reflected or bounced off the object. With the creation of the light, colors have been a part of God's sovereign design since the beginning.

Although the ancient Hebrew language had no specific word to translate the property of light that we currently call "color," we know that they saw color and attributed significance to specific colors. One of the greatest displays of God's creativity and regard for colors is in the Exodus account of how He directed the design, construction and decoration of the Tabernacle. Every piece of furniture and textile was an expression of His divine character. As the instructions were given for the decorations and furnishings of the tabernacle, God was very specific about expressing Himself in the color choices. Particularly the curtains that lined the entrance.

> *And for the gate of the court shall be a hanging of twenty cubits, of blue and purple, and scarlet, and fine twined linen, wrought with needlework: and their pillars shall be four, and their sockets four.*
>
> Exodus 27:16

Then there is the rainbow. A rainbow is a display of several colors in the sky, formed when the sun's light is refracted and dispersed by rain or other atmospheric water. When we think biblically about the rainbow, most people stop at the rainbow seen in Genesis by Noah, after the flood. But there is also a rainbow that is above the very throne of God, to represent His eternal glory, as seen in

Ezekiel's vision. The bible is filled with color symbolism. Even the book of Revelation uses color to express or symbolize specific images. It is also filled with color references as a means of expressing various emotions. These color references are used to reveal certain truths.

Much like biblical revelation and color, great brands and color work hand in hand. This is because color offers an immediate method for conveying a message or meaning without using words. Used properly, the right color can evoke emotion, express feelings, grab attention and trigger a specific response. Our brains have been hardwired to respond to colors differently. For example, the combination of red and white colors causes our brains to pause and pay attention. This is the reason why the stop sign uses these colors. If the stop sign were green and white, it might suggest a different action. With this knowledge in mind, Target stores strategically use the simplicity of the red and white colors in their branding. However, these color responses may also differ slightly, based on culture and region. While most color psychology is consistent, it is important to have an understanding of how your target audience views colors culturally.

Research shows that people make up their minds within ninety seconds of their initial interactions with either people or products. Approximately sixty to ninety percent of a person's decision to select one brand over another is attributed to color. So strategic use of colors can contribute to differentiating products from competitors and influencing moods and feelings, either positively or negatively.

When humans see color, a set of thoughts develop in our minds. Proper color selection can facilitate brand recognition and foster brand equity. It is important for any branding process to include an awareness and understanding of color psychology into the branding process. Color Psychology is the study of how hues affect human behavior. Color can influence perceptions that are not always obvious. Even the taste of food is influenced by the color of the food. Most high-end restaurants serve food with bright and colorful appearances on the backdrop of a white plate, to trick the mind into thinking that the food is more appetizing.

Color is the visual component people remember most about a brand. Many of the most recognized brands like UPS and Coca-Cola rely on color recognition. Color increases brand recognition by up to 80 percent. *(Source: University of Loyola, Maryland study)* Branding professionals understand that color makes a brand stand out, therefore they follow the principles of color. The strongest of brands can be easily identified by the consistency of their color usage.

Now that you have a general understanding of the importance of colors in branding, we will take a deeper look in the psychology of colors. This section will help you to understand how you can use color in your brand to express your brand message. You will no longer select colors just because you think they look nice, but you will begin to apply strategy and theory behind your color selections.

The basic principles of color theory are built upon three groups of colors – primary secondary and tertiary. These groups are then used to create various color schemes like analogous, complementary and nature.

Illustration 5.5 **Color Wheel**

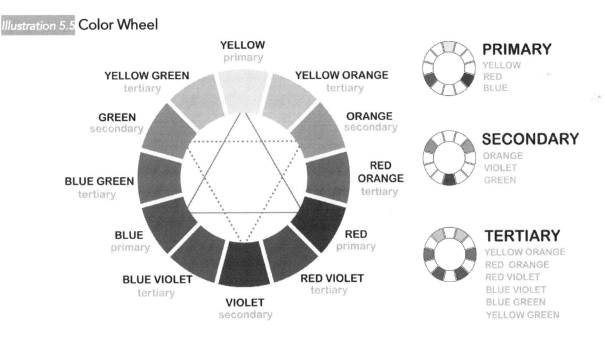

Primary Colors

Primary colors are the three main colors of the color wheel that are then mixed with each other to create the secondary colors. Primary colors are red, blue and yellow. These colors are considered primary colors because the pigments cannot be made from combining any other two colors.

Secondary Colors

Secondary colors are the colors that are created by mixing the three primary colors. For example, the secondary colors are orange, purple and green on the color wheel. The secondary colors are positioned on the color wheel between the primary colors.

Tertiary Colors

Tertiary colors are the result of blending primary and secondary colors together. On the color wheel, the tertiary colors are positioned between the primary and secondary colors. Yellow-orange, red-orange, red-purple, blue-purple, blue-green and yellow-green are all examples of tertiary colors.

When these collections of colors are used correctly you create color harmony. **Color Harmony** is the correct combination of colors that is attractive to the human eye. These colors are neither too intense nor too mild. It is important to select colors that create balance in your branding. The goal is to create something that is not to boring that it is overlooked, but not too bold that it becomes unpleasant.

Colors on the color wheel have significance and symbolism. We attribute certain emotions that influence behavior to colors. Brand managers select colors that reflect the emotions that they want their brand to represent. Below in Illustration 5.4, is a graphic display of the general psychology of colors. Each color on the color wheel has both an emotional or psychological trigger and a meaning or representation.

Illustration 5.6 Color Meaning

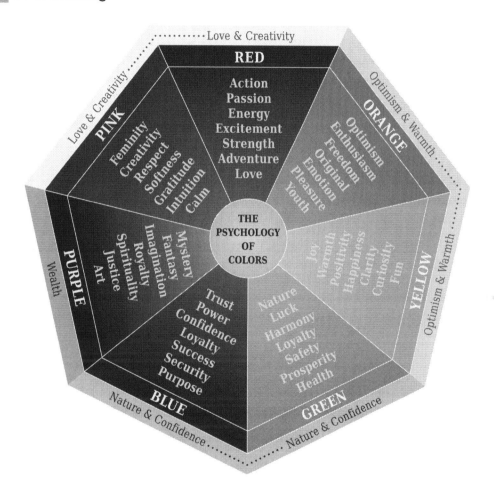

Pantone

Another great reference source for selecting colors to use in your design and branding is Pantone. The Pantone name is globally known as the standard method for color communication and matching for designers, manufacturers, retailers and customers. Pantone also established the Pantone Color Institute, a consulting service that forecasts color trends. They develop seasonal trends, custom color development and palette recommendations for products, designs and corporate identity.

Annually, the Pantone Color Institute releases the Pantone Color of the Year. These colors inspire and influence everything from fashion to furniture design. It is helpful for any organization that desires to remain current and relevant to use this reference as a resource for the development of their brand identity and communications efforts.

Colors should be chosen wisely. Effectively selecting colors to represent a brand requires more than choosing colors that look nice together. Brand builders must understand the psychology of color and how to use it strategically to communicate a brand message and story. When selecting colors for your brand, you should refer to the adjectives and feelings list that was created in chapter 1. Your brand colors should coincide with those adjectives and feelings.

Using Typography that Speaks

Typography is one of the most effective and ancient means of communication. But, before we fully dive into typography, let's take a look at how Merriam-Webster defines it:

> *"Typography is the style, arrangement or appearance of typeset matter."*

Typography is probably the most abused area of brand identity. Particularly because many individuals and organizations do not have a clear understanding of what it is, let alone, it's importance. It involves more than just picking a cool or pretty font. Effective typography also involves selecting typefaces, point sizes, line lengths, line spacing and letter spacing to communicate a message and evoke a desired emotion in the mind of the reader.

Typography can bring emphasis to important points that you desire to stand out. Just a simple act of increasing the size or boldness of a font can create a mood. Writing something by hand can be a display of personal communication. In the sixth chapter of the book of Galatians, the Apostle Paul proves this point by emphasizing that this section of the epistle was written in his own handwriting. In verse eleven, he points out that his large, hand-written letters bring emphasis to his point.

See with what large letters I have written to you with my own hand!
Galatians 6:11 (NKJV)

Paul's used his handwriting to bring genuineness and authenticity to the words that he was communicating.

Surprisingly, the font type used in your logos, designs and text also arouses different emotions. When used properly, with the correct spacing, size and color choices, typography can be instrumental in establishing an anticipated brand perception. These choices will help to set the visual tone of your design or document.

For the sake of avoiding a long drawn out section on typography, I will try to summarize the art and technique of typography.

There are basically five different categories of typefaces. Serif, Sans Serif, Script, Modern, and Display. With thousands of font choices, each category may inspire a variety of feelings, emotions and associations when viewed by a person. Depending on the nature of your project and design, it is useful to look for font choices that are beyond the limited fonts that come preloaded into your word processing system.

Serif Fonts

Serif Fonts are a category of fonts that include serifs. **Serifs** are the small lines or strokes at the ends of font characters. Although they can be very decorative, these small lines are used to connect the characters in the mind and make large amounts of text more readable. The eye is believed to travel more quickly across a line when a serif is attached to the characters. Serif Fonts are most often found in the body text of corporate documents, books, newspapers, and magazines. These items require exceptional legibility.

The feelings, emotions and associations generally conveyed by Serif Fonts are traditional, comfortable, reliable, and respectable. Examples of Serif Fonts include Times New Roman, Garamond, Baskerville and the list goes on.

Sans-Serif Fonts

Developed in the 1800's, Sans-Serif Fonts are a category of fonts that do not include the character extending feature of serifs. Sans-Serif fonts also generally have a thinner line width variation than serif fonts. These fonts appear more clean and stand out from the document. Sans-Serif Fonts are great when used in heading text, captions, advertising and charts and graphs.

The feelings, emotions and associations generally conveyed by Sans-Serif Fonts are modern, clean, stable and objective. Examples of Sans-Serif Fonts include Helvetica, Futura, Frutiger and ITC Franklin Gothic.

Script Fonts

Script Fonts are a category of typefaces that mimic the fluid stroke created by handwriting or calligraphy. They are most commonly used in invitations, announcements, and formal documents. However, depending on the style of the typeface, they can also be used casually for advertisements and brochures for documents that need a more casual look.

The feelings, emotions and associations generally associated with Script Fonts are creativity and elegance. Examples of Script Fonts include Vladimir Script, Edwardian Script, Linotype, and Bradley Type.

Modern Fonts

Modern Fonts are a category of typefaces that are designed in the style of the fonts that were created in the eighteenth century. During this time, improvements in paper and advanced printing techniques brought about changes in the typefaces of that time. These fonts are recognizable by their long horizontal and thin serifs and their lack of a slant on the letters. At large sizes, Modern fonts can be very eye catching.

The feelings, emotions and associations generally associated with Modern Fonts are stylish, progressive, chic and strong. Examples of Modern Fonts include Latin Modern, Dubiel and Rundfunk.

You should consider the moods and personalities of each font choice.

Display Fonts

Display Fonts are a category of typefaces used to grab the attention of the reader. They are designed to stand out and are usually more eccentric than the other typefaces. These fonts may appear to be shadowed, engraved, distressed or hand-tooled. Display Fonts are most commonly used as headers and in posters and signs.

The feelings, emotions and associations generally associated with Display Fonts are friendly, expressive, amusing and unique. Examples of Display Fonts include Algerian, Banco, Bauhaus and Umbra.

Your selection of font choices can say a lot about your brand. Just as our minds are trained to respond to color choices, we are also program with a set of responses to font choices. A legal document written in a Display Font may not appear to be valid or professional. Likewise, a children's ministry written in a Serif Font may not seem as appealing to kids. Much like the way that you selected the type of clothes you wear, based on the event, you should select your font based on the nature of your organization. Different occasions call for different clothing and different organizations call for different font selections.

More often than not, font choices set the tone for your design and communication. They can influence the viewers perception of your brand. The font selection should match the message or purpose of your brand and your design. Before you begin looking for fonts, you should start by reminding yourself of your desired brand feelings and emotions. From there, you should consider the context and the audience of your communication. While your logo may be fun and playful, you may not want the text of your contract documents to appear the same way. Most organizations choose a font for the logo, a standard font for headlines and a standard font the body copy (text inside the document, such a letters, forms and book paragraphs).

Combining fonts can be extremely effective, but it can also get a bit messy. Much like color choices, your font choices should complement each other and should not clash. Fonts should be different but not opposing. Finding

Fonts should be different, but not opposing.

the right font combination takes a thoughtful eye. You should consider the moods and personalities of each font choice.

Another thing to consider, is that unique font choices can be a bit expensive. I would only use a font that had to be purchased, if I were to use it in a logo or something that I wanted to trademark. Beyond that, there are plenty of sites that offer free font downloads. Just remember to always review the license and the terms of use before using the font. The correct font can as impactful as a graphic.

Using Pictures that Convey

Pictures are an immediate means for conveying a message. One image can instantly deliver a large amount of information because we can comprehend an image all at once, compared to reading which takes slightly longer to process. A single visual image can say several things. Vision is the primary source for all of our experiences.

This is why selecting the right images or photography is crucial to building your brand image. The human brain is wired to respond to visual images. It takes us less than 30 seconds to form an impression of someone or an organization. Selecting the right pictures and images are a great way to build and reinforce your brand. Quality imagery will also play an important role in communicating your brand personality and aesthetic. Pictures can be used to communicate a brand in several different forms, including billboards, websites, print advertisements and social media posts. However, there are three main areas that should be considered when selecting or creating photos to use in your branding. These are also the three biggest mistakes that organizations make when using pictures.

Three Keys to Selecting Images

There are three key things to consider when building your brand imagery. Those keys things are image quality, selecting stock photography and booking photographers.

Image Quality (Resolution)

When selecting pictures or photos, it is important to first consider the communication vehicle that you will be using. Images being posted online require a lower resolution than images that are to be used in printed documents. Resolution in design refers to the sharpness and clarity of an image. Most online images are set to approximately 75ppi and printed images should have a resolution of about 300ppi. **PPI** is an acronym for Pixels Per Inch. Which indicates the number of pixels used for every inch of a digital image. The higher the PPI, there will be more detail and clarity in an image. Most online sites and documents will use a lower PPI, to allow for faster loading times. However, printed documents look better at a higher PPI because they do not have to load and may be viewed longer by the audience.

PPI is often confused with **DPI**, which is the acronym for Dots Per Inch. Pixels Per Inch and Dots Per Inch are not the same. Dots Per Inch refers to the quantity of ink dots for every inch of a printed image. DPI considers the printer image, while PPI considers the digital image. The image below illustrates the difference between low PPI images and higher PPI images.

> Pixels Per Inch and Dots Per Inch are not the same.

Too often, organizations make the mistake of finding images online, by using a search engine. They then use these images in their printed promotional documents, but when the documents are printed, they generally produce an image where the viewer can see the individual pixels that form the image. This is called **pixelation** and it happens because the resolution was too low. Pixelated images being used in your brochures and printed advertisements communicate a lack of professionalism and quality.

The illustration below displays the amount of detail in an image, based on pixel quantity.

Pixels Per Inch

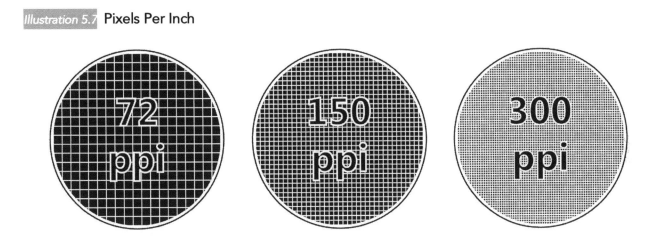

Stock Photos

To have a visually appealing website or an attractive brochure, you need photos. Photos can attract the attention of an audience, but more importantly, photography can help to communicate a message quickly. The problem with photos is that most people don't have quality photos that are readily available, so they turn to stock photos. **Stock Photos** are a collection of photos, vectors, or illustrations that you can license by paying a fee or subscription to the author, to use the images in a variety of ways.

Stock Photos are available for several different uses and are generally less expensive than to hire a photographer and studio to produce quality images of your own. They not only save you money, but they also save you time. It is more convenient to use an image that is already created, when you have a quick document to create or website update. A designer can browse thousands of high-quality images of virtually any subject matter, download it, and use it in their graphics.

There are several sites for finding stock photography, but here are a few of the most popular sites to use:

- www.gettyimages.com – A selection of images, videos and sound clips
- www.istockphoto.com – A selection of images, illustrations and video clips
- www.stock.adobe.com – A selection of images, illustrations and video clips

The problem with stock photos is that many organizations grab photos that are obviously generic. There are some stock images that appear so commercialized that a viewer will immediately spot that the image is not authentic. Another problem with stock images is that ministries and organizations tend to grab images that are not an honest representation. I have seen several church websites that host images of racially ambiguous people and families. Or very hip and young people smiling and hugging. All of this is great, until you visit the organization and there is no one that resembles the images. I understand the desire to appear like the people that you desire to attract, but when those people come and don't see anyone that looks like them, your brand has built a reputation as a liar. You begin to lose the trust of your audience.

If you must select stock photos, take care to use the ones that most accurately depict the current state of your organization.

Photographers

Having a photographer to produce authentic and quality images of your services, events, members or clients is an absolutely essential component to your branding success. As technology evolves the resources for amateur photographers have increased, but investing in quality still photography equipment and experienced photographers are worth it. Debauched photography is the pictorial equivalent to poor writing and typos in a professional document. If you would be embarrassed by either of those, you should be just as concerned about the photography that represents your brand. A photographer can build a consistent brand look that can be reflected across your printed and online presence. Developing original photography will also help your brand stand out from other brands in your industry.

> Debauched photography is the pictorial equivalent to poor writing and typos in a professional document.

Quality images tell your audience that you take your ministry, organization or business serious. The quality of your images communicate the quality of what you offer. Building trust will help them build the confidence to invest their time or money. A professional photographer will understand how the right lighting, composition, retouching and styling will translate in a photo, to tell the visual story of your brand. Professionals will also know how to come up with new and creative ways to connect with busy and distracted audiences.

When searching for a photographer, you must do your research. We live in a time when anyone can pick up a camera and call themselves a photographer. There is a high risk for failure when hiring a photographer that you don't know. Never hire a photographer whose work you have not personally seen. Most professional photographers should have an online portfolio to display some of their work. Its best to review the portfolios for photos that reflect the style that you seek to represent your brand.

There are several different types of photography styles and photographers generally specialize in specific style categories. Having a least a basic knowledge of the style that best fits your brand identity will help you when selecting a photographer. Conduct your research to know what style will work best. This will also help to ensure that your brand stands out and is consistent.

Below is a list of common photographer specialties and styles:

- **Still Photography**
  These photographers are good for product, packaging and still life photo shoots.

- **Food Photography**
  These photographers are good for photographing cuisine, cooking and restaurant environments.

- **Candid/Lifestyle Photography**
  These photographers are good for capturing live events or people in the moment.

- **Portrait Photography**
  These photographers are good for headshots and close-ups of people.

No matter what you desire to communicate or the nature of your organization, high quality photography is important to contributing to the overall success of your brand. Taking the time to find and hire a professional photographer to express your brand is essential. The right photographic images can be powerful and effective.

The right photographic images can be powerful and effective.

Using Videos that Inspire

Since its invention, video has become one of the most effective means for brands to reach broader audiences. People respond better to information that they can view and hear, rather than information that they have to read. With the development of the internet, video content has maintained its place as the dominant branding tool. Video content ranks higher on Google and other search engines. Creating online videos is an immediate way to reach a worldwide audience with a branding message that is both engaging and easier to retain. Web pages that incorporate video are known to convert 80% better than those without video. Building trust and becoming recognized as an authority in your niche, it is important to create video content that tells your brand story and inspires your audience to action.

Developing videos for the sake of doing them, without proper attention to quality and technique, will hurt a brand more than not using them at all.

The days of quality videos being reserved for only large organizations has been eliminated because the access to video cameras and tools are now more affordable. Additionally, the equipment and software has become easier for even the most novice producer. Today, it is extremely possible for even the smallest companies to create quality videos to communicate their brand. However, this wide spread increase in professional video production makes poorly developed videos even more apparent.

Creating effective brand videos go beyond simply hitting the record button on a mobile phone. Developing videos for the sake of doing them, without proper attention to quality and technique, will hurt a brand more than not using video at all. Poor quality videos can communicate a negative outlook on your organization and with the use of the internet, this outlook on your organization can go viral very quickly.

Regardless of the platform or equipment that you choose to use, it is important to ensure that your video content matches the brand quality that you want to display and that it contains the key components for effective brand communication.

Key Components of Brand Videos

To be effective, there are a few components that every brand video must include. Below is the list of those components.

- **A Story**
  Video is a way to humanize your brand and display personality. People can see your brand and find a point of connection. The use of video is ideal for generating emotion because the movement of the video grabs attention and combined with sound and facial expressions, force the viewer to pay attention. Before you start filming or planning any video footage, it is important for you to have a clear understanding of the emotional crux of your brand's story. The intent of the video should be strong. Every following decision and choice for the video should reference to that story.

> **Before you start filming or planning any video footage, it is important for you to have a clear understanding of the emotional crux of your brand's story.**

Throughout time, humans communicated with the use of storytelling. Most of the bible is expressed through the telling of stories and the experiences of other humans. Families pass down stories of their ancestors. We get children to learn information by telling stories. The stories that are remembered the most are the stories that appeal to the emotion of the listener. Brands that successfully learn how to show who they are, become the brands that are most remembered.

- **Brand Voice and Personality**

  You have previously defined your brand voice and personality and now you are ready to produce a brand video. Your brand video should be your brand personality in action. Building a brand voice in your video means that every video must have a consistent tone and appearance. Uniformity in lighting, atmosphere and angles all communicate the brand personality.

  A great way to express your brand voice and personality is creating or locating video visuals and sound that reflect your brand. You shouldn't just limit your brand's identity to print ads and materials, but the colors, look and feel that you identified for your brand should also be displayed in your video content. The music, voice overs and editing pace that you use should also convey this same personality.

- **Audience Engagement/Call to Action**

  An effective brand video should include audience engagement or inspire them to take a specific action. Your video should invite them to like or follow you on social media, visit your website, subscribe to your mailing list, make a purchase or attend your event. It is helpful to keep your videos short enough that people don't log off or move on before hearing your call to action.

Ways to Use Video to Communicate Your Brand

Video is one of the most effective means for communicating your brand because of its ability to quickly grab the attention of the viewer and its widespread reach. However, many organizations lack the creativity to consistently develop fresh content or subject matter that will keep the attention of the target audience. Generally, they run out of content and ultimately give up on developing video content. Below are a few types of videos that can be created to communicate your brand message.

- Webinars

  Webinars are online seminars. They can help build your reputation as an authority in your field. With proper implementation, they can help to boost your brand's credibility and prove to be useful to people seeking information. However, proper execution is important to filming a successful webinar. Details such as subject matter, on camera talent, promotional copy, and scripting all contribute to your webinar's success.

  An example of a webinar subject matter that a church could use may be "Who Needs Church Anymore?" This could be an attention getting title and the content could be persuasive enough to inspire a person to visit your church. While this subject could grab the attention of a vast audience, it is important to remember a few things.

  - On Camera Talent

    The person on the camera, hosting the webinar must be confident and articulate. The host must present themselves as a subject matter expert that is experienced and educated on the topic. They should also be a person that does not have a voice that could be annoying or too quiet. It should be someone that people would want to listen to.

  - Audience Takeaway

    When developing your webinar content, it is important to consider 'how will my audience benefit.' Your video must not seem like a sales pitch or just another church invitation. The audience should gain a level of insight that will cause them to take action and share your content.

- Behind the Scenes Videos

  When your team is planning an event or on set, including a behind the scenes look at the planning and processes can build excitement around your brand. Audiences love an inside look at what goes on behind the doors of an organization. A social media live video could be a great way to inspire your audience. This also displays the hard work and planning that you have invested in your organization and could inspire your audience to also invest.

- Vlogs

    A **Vlog** is a blog where the content and postings are primarily in video form. In essence, a vlog is a video version of a blog. Vlogs are another great way to build your brand because they can display the personality of your organization and also provide some valuable information for your viewers. Vlogging is also more personal than other videos. While lighting and sound are still important, a vlog doesn't require a studio quality. They should feel informal and personal. Also, through a vlog, you can address specific topics that your audience desires to learn more about. A vlog can be constructed like a video FAQ (Frequently Asked Questions) or a How-To Video.

- Testimonial/Influencer Interviews

    An easy way to build trust for your brand is to host a testimonial video or an interview with an industry influencer. Featuring profiles of your staff, members or beneficiaries explaining their experiences and why they trust your organization makes for intriguing content. Even more effective is partnering with industry influencers. Industry influencers are individuals that your audience may consider experts in your field of business or organization. A characteristic of an influencer may be large social media followings and audience engagement.

- Live Video Streaming

  Live streaming has become a very useful tool for organizations. Particularly ministries who want to share their messages with a larger audience. Various organizations are now using live video to support their goals. Live videos are a way to make the organization feel more authentic. The

  Live videos are a way to make an organization feel more authentic.

  problem is that many organizations do not consider lighting, sound and camera angles when filming. Often times videos are dark, the sound is distorted and the camera is slanted or hand held by an operator who jumps and moves to frequently for the video to be enjoyed. Another thing that organizations should consider is the number of live viewers watching their videos. Social media sources like Facebook Live, display the number of people watching your video.

  With over 3.2 billion people with access to the internet (according to the International Telecommunication Union), it is disconcerting to have a video with an average of less than 10 live viewers. And even worse is a live video that displays crowd or audience shots of fewer than 10 people. The audience size communicates to the person who happens to come across your video that the information you are providing is not worth hearing or viewing. It is important to invest in properly promoting your live video before you go live and to ensure that the video quality is inviting enough for people to pause and watch. Anything less is a waste of time and could be considered negative advertising more than positive.

  - Live Video Stream Hosting

    Live stream provides an opportunity for you and your audience to interact and engage with each other. The audience can ask questions and someone from your team can respond and answer those questions. These interactive opportunities allow you to gain real-time insight into your audience's thoughts and views about your content and your organization.

There are a few great platforms that offer live stream hosting services. Some of the most popular sites are:

- Livestream.com
- Facebook Live
- YouTube Live
- Periscope
- Meerkat

Leveraging the Power of YouTube and Vimeo

Over 50 percent of mobile internet traffic is attributed to online videos. This reinforces the idea that a large part of your branding strategy should include online video content. Sites like YouTube and Vimeo allow you to upload your content to their sites for viewing by their large audiences.

- YouTube

  YouTube is the second most used search engine on the Planet. Over a billion unique site visitors view over six billion hours of video on this site, each month. There is approximately 300 hours of video uploaded to the site every minute. YouTube is an effective means for reaching a larger audience with video content and for building your status as an authority. In 2013, YouTube launched its free video streaming host, bringing live video to its billions of viewers. Below are a few tips to improve your video content on YouTube.

o **Shareable**

The success of video content on YouTube is its level of shareable information. The more likely people are to share your videos, the larger your reach becomes. Your videos should contain content that audiences will want to pass along to their friends. Videos that are short and to the point, with informative or entertaining information are more likely to be shared by others. A great approach is to appeal to their conscience, their interests, or their heartstrings. It is also important to make sure that your video doesn't feel like an infomercial. All of us feel like we see too many ads every day. Viewers want to gain something out of the content and not feel like they are being brainwashed. You will have to create videos that promote your brand without being too preachy or sales focused.

o **Search Engine Optimization**

Search Engine Optimization (SEO) is the process of including targeted keywords in your tags, titles and descriptions of any online content. These are words that people are likely to enter into Google, when searching for information. For example, if you own a nail salon, you may want to include keywords like "manicure," "acrylic," or "designs." Even entering the city where your organization is located will associate your content with people looking for your services, in your city. Put yourself in the shoes of the person who might search for a video like yours. "What keywords will they enter into a search engine?" YouTube is owned by Google, so the more you include SEO into your videos, the more probable you are to show up higher in the results list.

- ○ **YouTube Cards**

  By adding YouTube Cards to your videos, you insert interactivity to your videos. Depending on the type you choose, these clickable cards can include a call to action, image, title or a link to a specific URL. With a click, your audience can be immediately directed to your website.

Know Your Audience

We talked about the importance of defining your brand audience in previous chapters however, I want to take some time to discuss the importance of having a clear picture of your viewing audience for video production. When developing a video branding strategy, it's important to consider your viewing audience and how they may view and use video content. All too often, people usually develop video projects that are geared towards a general audience. The problem with this one-size-fits-all approach to video production dilutes your reach.

It is important to tailor your video for the viewing preferences that your ideal audience may have. Not everyone is attracted to or moved by the same images, sounds and graphics. Without a strategic look at these things, you leave the success of your production to chance. Knowing the ideal viewing preferences of your audience will assist you in making decisions like the type of music that will appeal to them, the on-screen talent that they can relate to, the background music that won't distract them, or the graphics that will not confuse or offend them.

> **Not everyone is attracted to or moved by the same images, sounds and graphics.**

Prior to any production planning, filming or editing, your ideal viewing audience has to be factored into the process first. Your videos will become more effective and gain a greater response if you map out who you endeavor to reach and the things that to which they are more likely to respond. The more insight you have on who you desire to reach, the more meaningful your content will become. A great tool to help you with specifying and learning more about your audience is Facebook Audience Insights.

- **Facebook Audience Insights**
  This business tool developed by Facebook is designed to help brand communicators and marketers learn more about their target audiences, including aggregate information about geography, demographics, purchase behavior and more.

  Let's say that you want to open a church in Chicago. You can select "Chicago" for location, and under "Interests," select "Christianity." Facebook will reveal the average age of its Chicagoan users who are interested in Christianity. It will also provide you with details about the genders of that market. One of the most valuable pieces of information is the estimate that it provides for the size of the market. This will let you know approximately how many Facebook users you could possibly reach with your video campaign.

  When using this tool however, it is important to remember that the information is based on the self-reported data and behaviors of Facebook users. It should not be treated as your only and final source of strategic information. If your audience aren't typically Facebook users, then this tool may not be useful to you.

Know Your Budget

It is always important to consider your budget when embarking on a video project. The type of video content you choose, the equipment and the hosting selections all depend on your budget. You also can't rely on people sharing your videos alone. In order to expand your reach, you will need to purchase some social media sponsored ads. It is important to have a clear understanding of what you can afford and how those funds will be allocated.

One thing to keep in mind is that video production budgets change depending on the specific project. You can't use the same budget amount for each project. Some projects may require more equipment or production expenses than others. Additionally, if you don't already own quality equipment, your initial video production costs may be higher than the subsequent costs, as you will need to spend money to acquire the equipment.

In-house video production will keep your budget low and increase your profitability. However, if you don't have a team of experienced videographers and designers or the scope of work exceeds your teams experience level, you have the option of hiring external vendors. Even if you hire externally, it is even more imperative that you are aware of the amount that you can afford to spend. I will give you a general listing of the budget breakdown for internal video production expenses, to help you plan your own production.

There are three categoric breakdowns for video production budgeting, namely pre-production, production and post production.

- **Pre-production**
  Pre-production budget items are all of the things that are done before you ever hit the record button. These things include the purchasing of any camera or lighting equipment, script writing and location expenses.

- Production

  Production budget items are all of the studio or in-field expenses for producing the video. These production items may include costuming, makeup, staffing, voiceovers and engineering.

- Post-production

  Post-production expenses are the items and the tasks that are done after the video has been recorded. These items can include editing, still and motion graphics and promotion.

Set your Content Apart

Video development may appear intimidating for beginners, but with proper planning, it can be an effective way to reach a larger audience and stand out from the online content clutter. The bad part is that everyone knows that videos are efficient, so they all are making them. However, most branding amateurs are not producing quality videos that stand out. Many times, the video production is subpar and not well strategized. These videos are often lost in the shuffle or "scroll" and not really watched by anyone.

Below are a couple of things to keep in mind when trying to produce video content that will stand out from the noise.

- Inform, Don't Sell

  Making the audience feel as if the video is informing or educating them, will help to create value. You must display and show your skill, talent and expertise in a way that will make the audience believe that you are an authority in the field. Starting your video by selling or immediately demanding an action is much like trying to get someone to marry you, before getting to know them. It just doesn't feel comfortable and most likely won't get the desired response. The more you build the value of who you are, the more inclined people are to make a decision in favor of your organization. Webinars on a specific subject matter related to your brand are a great way to inform and educate your audience. Once you get to pitching the sale, the commitment becomes easier when they audience trusts your brand as an authority. Webinars are a simple way to build that trust. There are several platforms that offer free and low-cost tools for hosting your webinars.

- **Take Risks**
  Doing something completely unorthodox or risky in your videos will help to grab the attention of your audience. The videos that look like all of the rest and play it safe will seldom get noticed or stand out from the others. When you want to get noticed by a larger audience, you have to take a risk and shock them will fresh content. Creating a Content Risk Matrix, is a great way to visually plan out your video production risks. This matrix can be used to choose the right mix of video risks to take. The chart below details a content risk matrix, the goal is to fit into the top, right box by being risky enough to stand out, but safe enough to appeal to a large audience.

Chart 5.2 Content Risk Matrix

RISK ↑	High Risk, Complicated, Offensive Content	High Risk, Viral, Appealing to a Mass Audience Content
	Mediocre, Common Content	Extremely Safe, No Risk Content
	SAFE →	

Your goal should produce content that will both inform people of your brand and have a great potential of going viral. Be careful not to take risks that aim at simply offending people but take risks that make your brand stand out in a positive manner.

Activity 5 *Create a Content Risk Matrix*	Start by drawing a large square, divided into four, like the one in Chart 5. On the outside of the boxes, along the vertical axis, write the word "risk," with an arrow pointed upwards. Then on the outside of the box, along horizontal axis write the word "safe," with an arrow pointed to the right. Starting with the box in the bottom left, write all the video ideas that you can think of, that are most common in your industry. In the box just above that one, write all of the craziest most risky, attention grabbing video ideas that you can think of. From there, jump to the bottom box on the far right some video ideas that are safe, that won't stir any offense or cause any risk of being misinterpreted. Lastly, in the top write box, using all of the ideas from the previous boxes, make a list of video ideas that are a combination and adaptation of the other ideas, avoiding being offensive or too common, or too safe. Then end result should be a list of video ideas that are neither offensive or safe but are relatable enough to grab attention and risky enough to go viral.

"The best brands communicate louder than the noise."

– Mike Martin, Author of The Ministry of Branding

As we have previously established, everything communicates. Organizations must have a strong plan for communicating on the outset. You must give direction, guidance and language to your voice. Having a clearly recognized brand voice creates a coherent vision and maintains consistency in internal and external communications.

Even amongst the noise of an overly saturated society, your brand's voice should be clear.

Just like the human voice, brand voices vary in tone, accent and cadence. Your brand's voice should be so distinct that if we removed your organization name from your website content, blogs, graphics, letterhead, business cards, staff and even your buildings, a person should be able to still link these assets to your organization. Even amongst the noise of an overly saturated society, your brand's voice should be clear. The best brands communicate louder than the noise. It takes commitment to develop a voice that resonates with your audience.

There are several factors that aid in establishing a brand voice and while there are many more, I will focus on four elements that I think are essential. Giving attention to your writing style, training the people who represent your brand, establishing culture within and around your organization and being intentional about the customer/visitor experience are the most influential in clarifying a brand voice.

Writing with Intent

When writing online content, it is important to first consider the intention behind your users search for information. Although you embed keywords into your website, it is important to also write content that will rank on search engines such as Google. Branding professionals must also write content that appeals to the search efforts of your audience. Content that is Search Engine Optimized is important to all of your branding strategy. Search engines are one of the most primary ways that your audience will discover your brand. You must invest time in the beginning to not only focus on the look and layout of your site, but you must also be intentional about planning your content.

You must also consider the action that you want the audience to take. After your content has ranked on the search engine and the user has clicked on your site, take time to think about what you want them to do or discover next.

Some examples of what they may do are:
- Joining a mailing list
- Order a product or service
- Subscribe to a service
- Attend an event
- Download a resource
- Share a link
- Provide you with information
- Make an educated life decision

Other things to consider when writing with intent are, is there a demand for the content that you are providing, the syntax that your audience uses and your competitions content. You should use words that your audience would likely use when searching for information. Don't just use words that sound deep or interesting to you, but your content should relate to the audience. Well written content will improve your brand strategy and your audience response.

Developing Brand Ambassadors

For years, companies and organizations have chosen brand ambassadors to be the "face" of their brands. Brand ambassadors are the human representation of a brand and are responsible for socially promoting the organization. Their work includes going out, meeting new people and introducing them to the brand. They will represent the organization at specific events and they may even perform product demonstrations or taste tests. The brand ambassadors job is to be the ideal representation of what the brand represents, how it looks and how it acts.

> **Most importantly, trust and credibility are paramount to being an outstanding brand ambassador.**

To be a successful brand ambassador, one must have a clear understanding of the organization that they represent. They must also be aware of and identify with the principles that are important to the brand. Most importantly, trust and credibility are paramount to being an outstanding brand ambassador. The organization has put their stamp of approval on the ambassador and entrusts them to represent the brand. There is no "off the clock" time for brand ambassadors. They represent the brand at all times. Whether they are attending a formal event, or speaking with someone while shopping, a brand ambassador is always expected to engage with people and represent the brand in a positive way. The more successful a brand ambassador becomes at representing a brand, the option for taking the brand off, becomes less likely.

Ambassadors Don't Just Represent Themselves

Brand ambassadors don't just represent themselves. Their lifestyle and actions are also a direct representation of the brand they promote. Several years ago, Subway took on a brand ambassador to promote what was called the Subway Diet. His role was to communicate how he lost weight by eating primarily food from the sandwich chain. Here was a man who went from weighing 420 pounds to 245 pounds on a diet centered around Subway. For a time, the commercials and pictures of his transformation helped to establish trust in Subway and in the ambassador. The company experienced so much success and growth from this relationship that a few years later, they boosted the ambassadors profile by launching a foundation named after the man and focused on teaching kids about the dangers of obesity and how to live a healthy lifestyle.

Fast-forward about fifteen to sixteen years later, and the sandwich chain announced that they have suspended their relationship with the brand ambassador as a result of an investigation into allegations of the man participating in child pornography. At the time of the suspension, the FBI was only investigating and no charges had been filed, but it was important for Subway to separate from the personal life of this ambassador. This man forgot that even his personal lifestyle was a reflection of the brand.

Jesus' Ambassador (Disciple) Model

In Chapter 2, we talked briefly about selecting your team. Jesus selected a team of twelve disciples to be his brand ambassadors.

> *All this is from God, who through Christ reconciled us to himself and gave us the ministry of reconciliation; that is, in Christ God was reconciling the world to himself, not counting their trespasses against them, and entrusting to us the message of reconciliation. Therefore, we are ambassadors for Christ, God making his appeal through us. We implore you on behalf of Christ, be reconciled to God.*
>
> 2 Corinthians 5:18-20

These twelve men walked closely with Jesus to learn his vision and mission. He took time to train and develop them to carry out his brand to the world.

Creating a Culture and a Movement

Your brand is the byproduct of the culture you create. The best way to protect your brand is to first protect your culture. **Culture** can be defined as the dominant pattern of learned and shared rules, beliefs, ideals and standards for shaping behavior, language, practices and understanding of a group of people. Culture is developed and transmitted by people, consciously and unconsciously; intentionally and unintentionally. It is the invisible bond which ties a people together. If you don't make a deliberate effort to sculpt the culture of your organization, your most dominant people and departments will craft it for you. Ultimately the dominant or popular culture will establish your brand. Good or bad, your culture is always in full play. Our cultural values shape our thinking, behavior and personality. These values influence our perceptions.

> Your brand is the byproduct of the culture you create.

Culture is not learned through vocalization. Culture has to be experienced. People learn the culture of your organization through touchpoints and experiences. The intentional development of consistent and unique experiences will create your culture. As your culture begins to influence the environment outside of your organization, that influence creates a movement. A movement is a group of people working together to advance their shared ideals and experiences. Ultimately, this should be the goal of every ministry and organization that desires to influence the world.

Culture is displayed and amplified by the actions words and deeds of the leaders. It is actuated in the structure of your organizational practices and processes. Culture is visible in all relationships of the leaders, staff, volunteers, members, visitors and customers. Most importantly, it is grounded in the shared practices, values, beliefs, languages, practices, stories and goals of those individuals. Although many small things contribute to culture creation, it spreads through an organization quickly. If a few leaders within an organization arrive late to work each day, the other staff and volunteers will arrive late. Very quickly, everyone within the organization will adapt this behavior and a disregard for timeliness will become the culture of that organization.

Intentional focus on creating culture will help to build and establish your brand.

A few keys to creating a culture are:
- Know your culture
- Communicate your culture
- Correct erroneous culture
- Celebrate and live your culture

Know Your Culture

As the leader of an organization, it is important that you understand and are clear about your current culture and the culture that you desire to create. If your organization is already established, it is your responsibility to educate yourself as much as possible about the current culture. Even if it is not possible for you to interact with the details that make up your culture, it is the responsibility of the leader to put people in place who have the ability to inform them of the details. If your organization is new, it is still your job to know the culture that you want to create. You should know the characteristics that your staff and team should have, this will help you in hiring the right people.

You must take the time out to know the things and the people that establish your culture. The best way to do this is to put yourself in the customer's point of view. Walking through every area that the customer may experience will give you a clear picture of your environmental culture. To get an understanding of your people culture, you can either hire secret shoppers to interact with your staff unsuspected or conduct surveys. Brand builders must make an effort to create environments and build a team of people that reflect the culture you desire to communicate.

Communicate Your Culture

Communicating the culture that you desire to create is a must. Your team or staff should not have to guess about your vision or culture. It must be communicated and recommunicated on a continual basis. Culture has to be ingrained in the hearts and minds of the people who represent your brand that they begin to communicate and express your values without thinking about it. The vision must not only be who the brand is, it must also be who they are.

Always train your people on the vision and culture of your brand. Communication is essential to creating buy-in to the vision. To ensure that culture is ingrained in the minds and hearts of my team, I put them through a quarterly Culture Course. In these courses I train them on the vision and culture of the organization. Some organizations begin by communicating the vision and culture at new hire and volunteer trainings. Others host events and activities to remind them of culture. You can never over communicate vision and culture.

> Always train your people on the vision and culture of your brand.

Correct Erroneous Culture

Culture by default must be avoided at all costs. If your organization is not new or a startup, and if you haven't been intentional about communicating culture, it is highly likely that a negative culture has already been created by default. However, if your company is new or has an overall good culture, regardless of the training you have provided your team, there may be individuals and occurrences that misrepresent your culture. You must determine the behaviors that exist and are harmful to your brand and culture. When these individuals and things happen, it is important that you immediately correct them. The immediate correction of erroneous behavior is a must. The longer culture conflicting people and occurrences are allowed to exist, the harder it will become to shift culture in the right direction later.

Celebrate and Live Your Culture

One of the best ways to reinforce correct culture is to celebrate it. Creating the culture is about the day-to-day interactions of your staff and customers. When someone gets it right, it should be praised and supported. Great leaders recognize and reward the people who involved in effectively displaying the culture that you intend to display within your organization. When they are celebrated, people are more likely to feel included in the vision and will become more committed displaying character that supports it. Offering bonus' and small gifts or gift cards to employees who receive highly rated customer survey cards is an easy way to acknowledge and reward employees exemplify the culture. Another way to celebrate culture is to publicly acknowledge the individuals who perform well. This can be achieved through an email communication to the entire staff, acknowledging the work of the staff member. The more that the culture is celebrated, the more likely people are to live the culture, even when they don't think anyone is watching.

Changing an Existing Culture

It's never easy to change or shift an existing culture. In many instances, the people in your organization have been operating with the same beliefs and behaviors for several years and trying to shift or change these habits will surely prove to be difficult. That is why it is important to always be mindful of your organization's culture and to never slack on enforcing it.

While changing an existing culture can prove to be a challenge, it is not impossible. If you are committed to doing the work, it is possible to bring people back to the things that your organization values. A great place to start, is with your frontline. The frontline is the team of people who most frequently interact with your customers and visitors. These people should be the persons in your organization who most consistently represent your values. Never keep a person that doesn't embody the culture that you want to create, on the frontline.

Another way to improve an existing culture is to show your team where they fit in the vision of the organization. When they see themselves as an important piece in the vision, they are more inclined to have vision buy-in. People who have vision buy-in will not only embody the culture but they will also help to enforce and improve the culture.

Creating Experiences that Support Your Brand

Every business or organization has an atmosphere. Although there is no physical building, even online retail shops have atmosphere. Some create it deliberately and some never even stop to think about how they are communicating through atmosphere. The atmosphere of their organization is so important that as a part of their training, Starbucks trains each of their employees on the atmosphere and the experience they want created, every time someone encounters their brand.

We live in an age that requires intentional experience planning for every organization and at every touchpoint.

What is atmosphere? Atmosphere is a business or organizations most dominant intellectual or emotional environment or attitude, that dictates experience. We live in an age that requires intentional experience planning for every organization and at every touchpoint. There are so many people doing or selling the same thing, that the only thing that may set one apart from the other is how intentional they are about the experiences they create. Even grocery stores are becoming more intentional about their experiences, by having live piano players and onsite sushi chefs. Experience planning is key to building a lasting brand.

A consistent experience at every touchpoint will greatly improve the perceived value of a brand. Touchpoints are your brands places of customer or visitor contact, from beginning to end. By identifying your touchpoints, you ensure that your brand is consistent with every interaction. These touchpoints exist before, during and after a person makes a purchase from your brand. To make your experience leave a lasting impression, you must take your guests on an experience journey.

The keys to creating effective experience touchpoints are ensuring that they are hospitable, comfortable, consistent, relevant, understandable and accessible. If they don't meet these minimum standards, it is likely that a person will have a bad experience when encountering your brand. There are several things that affect atmosphere and experience, but below are a few to consider when establishing your brand.

Things that affect atmosphere and experience:
- Online and Physical Architecture
- Accessibility
- Environmental Graphics
- Music
- Smell
- Lighting
- Staffing/Volunteers
- Cleanliness

Considering these cultural elements will ensure that your customers, members or visitors have a positive and consistent experience which each interaction. This is how you build a brand experience.

Activity 6

Experience Touchpoints

Take a moment to write out each touchpoint that a guest may experience when encountering your brand. I have listed some below that may or may not apply to your brand, use the ones that apply and if you think of more, add them. If your organization already exists do the current touchpoints communicate your vision?

Touchpoints:
- Website
- Parking Lot
- Foyer/Waiting Room
- Hosts/Greeters
- Restrooms
- Seating

"Long-term consistency trumps short-term intensity.

– Bruce Lee, Actor, Film Director and Martial Artist

There are several benefits to maintaining consistency in your branding. One of the most important benefits is that consistency helps to build trust in your brand, with your audience. If every time they encounter your brand and receive the same level of service, quality and overall experience, your audience will become loyal to your brand and recommend it to others. Another reason why consistency is important in brand building is that it makes your brand easily recognizable. Brands that have consistent imagery and design are recognizable, even if they never display their name or logo. Great examples of this are companies like Apple and Target. Consumers have been subconsciously trained on the brand identity of these companies that when they see the commercial advertisements for these brands, they know who is doing the advertising, before the logo is ever displayed. Apple is true to its simple and clean imagery as much as Target is true to their brand's use of whites and reds. A key goal of every brand that desires to be great, should be to create consistent experiences. These experiences should become so synonymous with your brand name that when audiences hear your brand name, they mentally start thinking of their next interaction.

> A key goal of every brand that desires to be great, should be to create consistent experiences.

Don't Misrepresent

An important factor to maintaining consistency is avoiding misrepresentation. The external brand identity that you create in advertisements, websites, printed graphics and social media should be the same brand they experience when they encounter your brand in person. If this level of consistency is not ensured, you will immediately loose trust with the audience. For example, if you are the owner of a restaurant and advertise on television, a happy and friendly wait staff, that must be the reality of the actual environment. Making promises or claims in your advertising, that are not the reality can even inspire litigation from consumers. Brands that don't monitor marketing presentation with real-world representation, will become labeled as liars, and brands that can't be trusted.

Establishing Branding Standards and Guidelines

Another way to maintain consistency is to establish branding guidelines. These guidelines are generally placed in a brand standards guide. This document sets the rules for the use of your brand assets, including your logos, colors, fonts and slogans. These guidelines may even define the tone and style of your brand language. All of the work that you have done in the previous chapters, to develop and create your brand should be documented. Your brand standards guide will keep your team consistent in their creation of business cards, websites, packaging and anything that represents your brand.

> **Another way to maintain consistency is to establish branding guidelines.**

When establishing your branding standards and guidelines, find a graphic designer to help you build your guide. The guide will explain branding standards for printed and online communication. Below are key areas to focus on with your designer and to include in your guide.

Elements of a Branding Standards Guide:

- **The Brand Story**
  The section should tell your mission, vision and brand values. This is where you explain to your team, what makes your brand unique and important. This should be a summary of your brand and not an overly worded document. Careful consideration should be applied to what to include.
- **The Logo**

The logo section should display the logo and the dos and don'ts of logo usage. Be sure to explain color and layout options for your brand.

- **The Color Palette**
  List the colors that support your brand, along with the CMYK and HEX codes for your brand colors.

- **The Fonts/Typography**
  Explain which fonts are used in your logo and the typeface that should be used in written branding items. You should also explain why these fonts were chosen.

- **The Imagery**
  This section should explain the types of pictures and images that should be used and how to display them.

- **The Voice**
  Lastly, the voice section should detail how your brand speaks and the types of words that should be used.

No matter how large or small your organization may be, your brand standards guide is a important tool. Once you have created your guide, your team should refer to them when planning all of your communication efforts. This guide will ensure consistency across all channels and touchpoints.

No matter how large or small your organization may be, your brand standards guide is an important tool.

Extending Your Brand

Once a brand has established a successful brand model and its position in the marketplace, it may consider branching out into other products and services. These products and services are often established as individual entities that are offshoots or sub-brands of the original organization. **Sub-Brands** are owned and closely tied to a larger parent company or original brand, but are still brands with their own identity. Successful brands have the power to apply their brand power to any industry and maintain consistency in quality and branding. Sub-brands generally build and sustain relationships with a new audience on behalf of the parent brand.

> **Successful brands have the power to apply their brand power to any industry and maintain consistency in quality and branding.**

In a business organization, a great example of the relationship between a parent company and its sub-brands is Disney who owns Disney Channel, Disney Theme Parks and the Disney Stores. These organizations are all owned by Disney but have their own operating practices. Although they are individual organizations, they all maintain and are consistent with the brand identity of the parent company. All of the Disney sub-brands share the same values and are easily identified as extensions of the main Disney brand.

In a ministry or church organization, examples of these sub-brands can be things such as youth ministries, men's ministries and other ministries in operation within a church. Many ministries are also extending their brands to community centers and record labels. At All Nations Worship Assembly, our children's ministry (ANWA Kids) and our record label (The Well Media Group) are both consistent with our brand values and identity. People should see the same brand qualities extended to your sub-brands.

Even if the products and services of your sub-brand are vastly different from the parent company, they should still hold similar brand qualities. The same brand perceptions that you were intentional about building earlier, should carry through to all of your sub-brands. The way you maintain this consistency across all brands is by creating brand standards that fit with the brand promise, identity and quality standards of the parent company.

Activity 7 *Build a Branding Standards Guide Outline*	Draft an outline for your Branding Standards Guide by listing the six sections that were detailed in this chapter. Under each section, list the branding choices that you decided on for your brand.

"No man was ever great by imitation."

– Samuel Johnson, English Writer

Avoiding Imitation Branding

With the vast amount of brands in every industry, it is important for brands to innovate their brand image.

The branding world is quickly shifting from innovation to imitation. Instead of creatively engineering new brands and taking the risk of trying something new, organizations have taken the languid approach. More organizations are finding brands that work and attempting to duplicate the "magic sauce." These brands generally do not last and the audience discovers the fraud in these types of companies, ultimately losing all trust. With the vast amount of brands in every industry, it is important for brands to innovate their brand image.

Innovating Over Imitating

The graphic designers that I work with, often complain of clients bringing them images of other brands and requesting to look and be like the brands in the images. The request to imitate is one of the most frustrating things for designers who endeavor to create authentic graphics. Every creative industry borrows from something previously created however, when establishing a brand, authenticity in important. Brands that imitate other brands in their look, feel and personality are no different than the knock off Louis Vuitton bags sold on street corners. These brands are cheap replicas that will never last or match the quality of the brand they impersonate.

There is a lot that you can learn from the branding efforts of successful companies in your industry. Learning why customers choose their brand can be helpful. The key is to be inspired to build and innovate based on your study of other brands, but never to duplicate their strategies or content. Your audience will notice the imitation and in the end, it will do more harm to your product or service than good. Furthermore, your competitors may notice the imitation and they might not sit by idle as you attempt to profit from their strategy.

Competitive Analysis

Conducting a competitive analysis should be the first step of every brand strategy. A **Competitive Analysis** is an evaluation of the strategic strengths and weaknesses of brands relative to your own product or service. This review should be completed, not to imitate your competitors but to discover what makes your product or service unique. Once you discover your unique advantage, your strategy should be to play-to or build on that strength. These things are what set you apart from your competitors. You should not be alarmed by the words "competitive" or "competitors." Every organization has competition. There are always things, businesses, and products competing for the desires and affections of your audience. It is advantageous to be aware of what is competing for your space in the minds and hearts of your audience.

> It is advantageous to be aware of what is competing for your space in the minds and hearts of your audience.

For churches and ministries, sin and corruption are not the only things competing for your audience. There are also other religions and false and corrupt doctrine. It is imperative for churches to be aware of "the church" that has either falsely captivated your audience as well as "the church" that has created a mistrust or disdain in the heart of your audience. This awareness will help you develop a competitive analysis that will help you brand your ministry in a way that will compel the audience to "trust-a-try" and visit or join your ministry. Your knowledge will help you to make more informed brand decisions.

The process of competitive analysis starts with identifying your competitors. Ask yourself, 'Who are the companies that offer a product, service or experience that is most similar to ours?' In simple terms, who would your customers choose if your organization was not an option? Once you have identified your competitors, identify and review their strengths and weaknesses in comparison to your own strengths and weaknesses. In the end, your brand strategy should highlight and promote your strengths. Delivering on these strengths will help you to build trust in the hearts and minds of your audience.

An easy way to view and conduct this analysis is to create a competition grid. Below is an example of a competitive analysis grid. Use the chart below to analyze your brand in comparison to your competitors. For each factor that I have listed below, honestly rate your brand on a scale of 1-4 with 4 being the strongest. Once you have rated your brand, do the same for the brands of your competitors. This will give you a clear picture of your weaknesses in comparison to your competitors.

Chart 8.1 **Competitive Analysis Grid**

Factor	My Brand Strength Rating	Brand 1 Strength Rating	Brand 2 Strength Rating	Brand 3 Strength Rating
Product				
Price				
Quality				
Service				
Reliability				
Expertise				
Stability				
Appearance				
Reputation				
Location				
Team				
Culture				
Relatability				

Establishing Brand Trust

One of the most important qualities of a brand is the level of trust that an audience has gained, in the brand promise. Building an audience that trusts your brands ability to deliver on your promise in each interaction with your brand is the cornerstone of effective branding. People need to believe that you are who you say that you are. The audience must be able to depend on the consistency of your brand's delivery.

Essentially, branding is about developing emotional connections with the people that you intend to reach. When choosing one bank over the other or one church over another, the primary drivers for behavior and decision making are the human emotions. Cognitive thinking does not drive product or service selection. Emotions are always at play in these decisions and the most powerful of all emotions, is trust. People support brands that they trust. Organizations must focus on three key elements to build brand trust.

Three key elements of build brand trust:

- **Brand Promise**
  To build and maintain trust, a brand must consistently hold true to its brand promise.

- **Brand Competence**
  To display competence and ultimately build trust, organizations must display attributes of success, reliability and expertise in their given field.

- **Brand Integrity**
  The reputation of a brand is key to displaying integrity and building trust. Integrity is established when a brand proves in action, to represent its spoken principles. Actions like offering refunds for bad products is a display of integrity.

Activity 8
Competitive Analysis Grid

Using Chart 8.1 as point of reference build a grid for comparing your brand with three of your competitors and rate each factor for your brand and the competitors from 1-4.

Be sure to be honest, this grid will display areas that you can improve and areas that you an highlight. Your strongest factors are the areas that you should highlight in your branding.

"The best investment is in the tools of one's own trade."

– Benjamin Franklin, Scientist, Inventor, Politician, Philanthropist and Businessman

Once you have established your brand identity, there are several tools available to help you build and spread your brand. Proper use of these tools will strengthen your brand and give it longevity in a modern society.

Implementing Trends without Becoming Trendy

There is a great difference between being relevant and trendy. Let's face it, trends come and go. It is important to know how to use trends without falling into the trap of becoming trendy. Brands that have not mastered the use of trends, without falling into the trap of becoming trendy will likely fade when the trend fades. However, trends are not all bad. The first step is to have a clear understanding of what a trend is. A **trend** is something that is popular during a specific point in time. Trends include everything from a style in fashion, entertainment and language. When used properly, trends can be successful tools to help promote your brand. Using trendy words, colors and images in your promotional graphics, apparel and marketing, will help your brand to appear relatable and current. However, using trends in your long-term branding is not a good idea. If you use a trendy font in your logo, or trendy words in your slogan, your brand will appear dated over time.

> Brands that have not mastered the use of trends, without falling into the trap of becoming trendy will likely fade when the trend fades.

The rule of thumb is to use trends in temporary promotions and branding and not in your long-term branding. No good brand wants to change its logo or slogan, every time trends change. However, the use of words, fonts, colors and images that speak to a specific generation, in a commercial or a short-term advertisement is a good use of a trend.

Using the Internet and Social Media to Reach an Audience

If the technology of computers and the internet had existed at the time that the apostles lived, I am sure they would have had websites and blogs. An online presence is the fastest and most cost-efficient way to deliver your brand to the world. The internet will become the most frequented road to your brand. The reality of our modern culture is that it is virtually impossible to run a business without having an online presence. When a customer or visitor wants to know your hours of operation, your address or any other general information about your brand; their first stop will be the internet and ideally, your website. There are key elements that should be included in your website and social media presence.

Website Elements

Websites are important for any organization. Many times, it is your one shot at making a first impression. People will judge the quality of your product and service based upon the quality of your website. While great design and written content play an important role in creating an effective website, there are also some key elements that should be included in your website.

- **Self-Hosting**

  The number one indicator of an unprofessional website is its URL. If the URL ends in something like blogspot.com and not the actual organizations name, people will not view your organization as a professional or quality entity. Custom domain names are not expensive to purchase and are worth the investment.

- **Business Address and Contact Information**

  The website is the first-place people will visit when they want to know the address and contact information of your organization. It is important to have this information clearly visible and accessible on your website. Also, adding your church location to Google Maps will also help improve how your organization appears in search engines.

- Navigation

  Navigation or navigation bars are like the "GPS" of your website. They are the links that get your website visitors to the information and resources that they need. Your website navigation should be easy to locate and understand.

Understanding Social Media Algorithms

Algorithms are a key component to social media and they will only expand and grow how they work, before they go away.

For the people who understand them, social media algorithms can be one of the best marketing tools of our time. However, if you lack an understanding of how algorithms work, they can be your greatest pain. **Algorithms** are a key component to social media and they will only expand and grow how they work, before they go away. Learning and understanding how they work would be in the best interest of any brand that plans to last.

Social media algorithms are the codes embedded into most popular social media platforms, that attempt to predict what their users like and enjoy viewing, based on their previous online activity. These platforms have tried to find a way to display the content that their users want to see the most. They do this by displaying the posts and ads from people and companies that the individual users engage with the most. This is why any brand that desires the effectively utilize social media, must have a strategy for engagement and making algorithms work for them. The more you get your audience to engage with your brand through social media, the more your brand will be displayed to them and people like them. The list below are tips on how to manipulate the algorithms to create engagement and give your brand more visibility.

Tips for Social Media Engagement:

- **Post Questions**

  One of the easiest ways to get people to engage with a social media post is to ask questions that will provoke a response. Posts that encourage people to comment, like, reply or share will appear more frequently online to people with similar interests. One brand that used this best is Mr. Clean. To increase audience engagement, they had the fictional character and their brand icon, Mr. Clean responding to user comments, no matter how crazy. People began commenting on the brands posts, just to see how Mr. Clean would respond. Ultimately, they boosted the visibility of the brand.

- **Use Tags**

  I say this with great caution. Tagging a person in a Facebook, Instagram or Twitter post will notify a user that they have been tagged in a post, which will ultimately cause them to go view the post. If the post is something they enjoy, the likelihood of them engaging with the post is high. The reason I use caution when recommending this action is that consistently tagging people in posts that don't apply to them or posts that they are not interested in, could have the adverse effect. People can become quickly annoyed by individuals who constantly tag them in random posts and they may be likely to delete the person or company that tagged them. However, if you tag a keynote speaker or someone connected to your brand, you will reach their audience and cause them to engage.

- **Ask**

  The easiest and most simple way to build engagement is to ask for it. It is not improper to ask your audience to like, share and follow your posts. With every video or post I encourage brands to ask for what they want. Sometimes people just need to be asked or reminded to do it.

Social Media Paid Advertisements

Social media advertising is targeted advertisements geared towards users on various social media platforms. These media platforms utilize user information to display highly relevant advertisements based on the users interactions with the platforms. Social media advertising can trigger high engagement with the target audience for a very low cost to

> **Social media advertising can trigger high engagement with the target audience for a very low cost to the advertiser.**

the advertiser. Most often, social media paid advertisements have a higher return on investment. These advertisements can be targeted to a very specific audience, based on the advertiser's preferences. Choosing paid advertisements over a simple post on your social media page, opens your advertisement to a larger audience and can expose your brand to more people.

There are four different types of social media platforms that offer paid advertising. There are social networking sites, microblogging sites, photo sharing sites and video sharing sites. Each type of site has a different focus and depending on the nature of your advertisement and the audience, one may be more effective than the other. Below is a detail of the types of social media sites and examples of each.

Four types of social media platforms:

- **Social Networking Sites**
  Social Networking Sites are online platforms that allow users to create a public profile and interact with other users on the website.
  Examples of Social Networking Sites:
    o Facebook *(www.facebook.com)*
    o LinkedIn *(www.linkedin.com)*
    o Google *(www.google.com)*

- **Microblogging Sites**

  Microblogging Sites are online platforms that allow users to exchange small elements of content such usually restricted to 140 -150 characters.

  Examples of Microblogging Sites:
  - Twitter *(www.twitter.com)*
  - Tumbler *(www.tumbler.com)*

- **Photo Sharing Sites**

  Photo Sharing Sites offer services such as uploading, hosting, managing and the sharing of photos publicly or privately with a limited amount of text content.

  Examples of Photo Sharing Sites:
  - Instagram *(www.instagram.com)*
  - Snapchat *(www.snapchat.com)*
  - Pinterest *(www.pinterest.com)*

- **Video Sharing Sites**

  Video Sharing Sites allow user to distribute their video clips online and involves the process of uploading, publishing and sharing.

  Examples of Video Sharing Sites:
  - YouTube *(www.youtube.com)*
  - Facebook Live *(www.facebook.com)*
  - Periscope *(www.periscope.com)*
  - Vimeo *(www.vimeo.com)*

The decision to purchase advertisements on a specific platform depends on the platform that your target audience prefers to use. See the Illustration 9.1 for a listing of the various social media platforms.

Illustration 9.1 Social Media Platforms

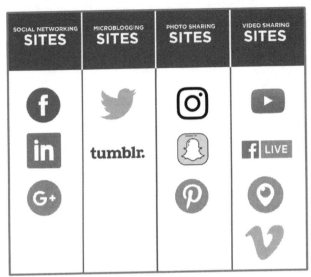

Activity 9 *Social Media Campaign*	Choose one social media platform that offers paid advertising. With the outline below, create a social media campaign for your brand.
	• Audit your current online social presence. What social media platforms are you currently active on? Which platforms bring the most value?
	• Define your campaign goals. For example, increase ticket sales and spread awareness for our church's annual men's golfing fundraiser.
	• Be specific and create the ideal target market using age, gender, beliefs, interests, education, etc. For instance, men who live in a 30 mile radius of Chicago, Illinois USA between the ages of 25 and 65 years of age who primarily use Facebook and are interested in golf.
	• Create a social media content calendar using photos, graphics, video and text that informs, educates and/or entertains your audience about the objective.
	• Track and analyze. Measure the success of your campaign using analytics tools such as reach, engagement, website clicks, sales, etc.

"Don't despise your season of preparation."

– Dr. Matthew L. Stevenson III, Author, Pastor, Businessman and Philanthropist

By now, you have spent a significant amount of time, resources and brain power to develop your brand and what it stands for. It deserves to be introduced to the world with an equally as strategized launch. Your brand launch is your one shot at a first impression, so it's important that you do it right. Even if you are relaunching an existing brand, it is imperative that you introduce it in a way that expresses your brand promise.

The Triumphal Entry of Jesus into Jerusalem is a direct example of a brand launch.

If we look again to the bible and more specifically Jesus, as a template for branding, we can't look beyond the way in which He launched His brand. After He trained and developed His team, he was ready to announce his brand to the masses. The Triumphal Entry of Jesus into Jerusalem is a direct example of a brand launch. This one encounter was so significant to the brand of Jesus that it is recorded in all four of the gospels. Matthew, Mark, Luke and John all saw this as a pivotal moment in the ministry of Jesus.

When they neared Jerusalem, having arrived at Bethphage on Mount Olives, Jesus sent two disciples with these instructions: "Go over to the village across from you. You'll find a donkey tethered there, her colt with her. Untie her and bring them to me. If anyone asks what you're doing, say, 'The Master needs them!' He will send them with you."

This is the full story of what was sketched earlier by the prophet: Tell Zion's daughter, "Look, your king's on his way, poised and ready, mounted on a donkey, on a colt, foal of a pack animal." The disciples went and did exactly what Jesus told them to do. They led the donkey and colt out, laid some of their clothes on them, and Jesus mounted. Nearly all the people in the crowd threw their garments down on the road, giving him a royal welcome. Others cut branches from the trees and threw them down as a welcome mat. Crowds went ahead and crowds followed, all of them calling out, "Hosanna to David's son!" "Blessed is he who comes in God's name!" "Hosanna in highest heaven!" As he made his entrance into Jerusalem, the whole city was shaken. Unnerved, people were asking, "What's going on here? Who is this?" The parade crowd answered, "This is the prophet Jesus, the one from Nazareth in Galilee."

- Matthew 21:1-11

The entry into Jerusalem was an announcement that the prophecy of Zechariah was fulfilled and that the King had come. Even Jesus' selection of the donkey as his ride was not just a fulfillment of Scripture, but also an illustration that a part of His branding was that He is the "Prince of Peace" as foretold by the prophet Isaiah. As horses were instruments of war, the donkey was the perfect animal for one who came to bring peace.

Even as Jesus confirmed His previous brand promises with the strategy of His launch, businesses and organizations must plan brand launches that complement their brand promises. If your promise is luxury and a grand life, you shouldn't host a launch that doesn't represent those same qualities. Every aspect of the launch must continue to communicate and reinforce the brand promise.

There are two audiences that you should consider when launching a brand, there is the internal audience. These are the people within your organization, who will represent your brand. Then there is the external audience, these are the people outside your organization, who will ultimately become the consumers of your products or services. Both launches require preparation and their own communications plan with release dates. In this chapter, we will review the process of launching a brand, both internally and externally.

Internal Launch

The internal brand launch is an integral part of the branding process that is often overlooked by many businesses and organizations. It's important that the people who will become your brand ambassadors are clear on your vision and are as excited about the presentation of the brand, as you are. No matter what industry you are in, the investment of your people is of great value. The aim is to create an emotional connection

> Knowing how to transform an employee or volunteer into a true brand evangelist or ambassador is the challenge.

between your brand and your employees or volunteers. Your team must be invested in the brand before you publicly launch. You have to inspire them to the point that they become your official brand evangelists, ready to tell the world about what you offer. Knowing how to transform an employee or volunteer into true brand evangelist or ambassador is the challenge. Below are some tips for planning an internal brand launch.

Tips for planning an internal brand launch:

- **Don't Get Ahead of Yourself**
  It's easy to get excited about the launch or relaunch of your brand by immediately changing email signatures, social media pages and websites. Don't get ahead of yourself, these changes should be made with proper consideration. You don't want to taint the reveal of your new brand. It is also not a good practice for your team to learn about or see your new brand image at the same time that the public

learns of it. Proper communication to your team about what is to come, prior to making these changes will help build the excitement in them.

- **Create an Internal Launch Calendar**
Setting a schedule for internal communication will ensure that you have given the proper amount of attention to sharing your vision and the value of your brand with your team. The Internal Launch Calendar will keep communications on track and timely. It will also prevent you from being tempted to get ahead of yourself by making public changes prior to the schedule. Be sure to include every step of the communication process and the exact communications being delivered.

- **Overcommunicate**
A simple, one-time email is not enough. It generally takes about six months for a brand or rebrand to be completely instilled in the minds of your target audience. Planning a series of emails that build upon the previous communication and that reveal more details about the new brand will help to effectively communicate what is to come.

- **Create a Frequently Asked Questions List**
No matter how frequently you communicate about your brand, prior to the launch day, there may still be some things that may be forgotten. Creating a "key points" or "frequently asked questions" reference tool for your team will ensure that they have a quick place to be reminded about the highlights of the brand.

- **Build a Champion Team**
Build a small team of key people to help communicate the brand launch and to help build excitement and team buy-in. This team will be the people to plan communication efforts and activities that will reinforce the brand vision into the

rest of the team. The champion team is your senior level leaders. It is a good practice to get your executives to buy-in before you start communicating with the rest of the team.

- **Create an Internal Newsletter**
  An internal newsletter that is only circulated to your team can be used to educate them on your brand, its promises, services, values and goals. You can also give them updates on the timeline of the external launch activities.

- **Create Branded Giveaway Items**
  You've spent a lot of time planning and developing your new logo and brand identity. Now it's time to show it off. Design and order a few branded promotional items to give away to your team. These items should have your logo and colors displayed very prominently. Be sure to avoid buying cheap useless items. Take the time and spend your money on items that people will use over and over again. These products will become a daily reminder of the brand and the brand promise.

- **Plan and Internal Brand Launch Event**
  A great way to build anticipation and garner excitement around your brand launch is to host a "big moment" launch event. It could be as simple as an exaggerated all staff meeting or lunch and learn, with a big reveal of the logo. Or you can go over the top, with a big launch party, just for the team. Either way, the internal brand launch event should be both informative and a rally or party.

No matter how you choose to launch your brand internally, making preparations to communicate with your team first, will ensure a successful role out. Making memorable moments and experiences will help to create internal buy-in and will motivate your team to take a hands-on approach to the external brand launch process.

External Launch

The time to go public with the launch of your brand is an exciting time. It can be as exciting and nerve wrecking as a couple finally making an announcement to family and friends that they are expecting a child. This is your baby and you have taken great care to ensure that preparations have been made for its arrival. The announcement or external brand launch is the final step of the preparations. You only get one shot at a first impression, so thinking strategically about how and when you want to make the introduction is important. Below are some tips for planning an external brand launch.

Tips for planning an external brand launch:

- **Build Anticipation of the Brand**
  Leading up to the launch day of your brand, you should build anticipation in your target audience with giving them teasers, without revealing too much. Building hype about your product or service is about giving the public small hints about what to expect. Apple is very good at releasing small possibilities about what their new phones may offer, without giving away too many details or any definitive information.

- **Create an External Launch Calendar**
  Much like the internal launch calendar, the external launch calendar will keep communications on track and timely. It will also prevent you from being tempted to get ahead of yourself by making public changes prior to the schedule. Be sure

to include in your launch calendar, every step of the communication process and the exact communications being delivered.

- **Synchronize your Communication Methods**
  Synchronizing your communications methods is an important step in launching a brand. You will need to examine the best ways to reach your audience and time each method. Below is a list of possible methods:
  - Outreach on Social Media
  - Email Campaigns
  - Videos
  - Announcements on your Website
  - Press Releases
  - Direct Mail
  - Launch Events

- **Focus on the People**
  When planning your brand launch, one of the most important elements you should employ is focusing your communication on the people you intend to reach. You should endeavor to show what your brand can do for people and how it can make their lives better. Avoid focusing on what they can do for your brand. Your audience and customers are focused on and interested in their problems and how your brand will fit into their lives. Every aspect of your brand launch should communicate how your brand can make their lives better.

- **Take Pre-Orders**
  Taking pre-orders or collecting pre-commitments to attend an event or purchase a service is an often overlooked strategy. Using your current contact list or

building a new list of contacts to make pre-orders is an effective way to launch your brand.

- **Plan the Event**

  To make your launch a lasting moment, it should be an event. If you choose to launch with a big event with keynote speakers and music, or if you chose a smaller more intimate event, this is your official announcement and it should represent what your brand stands for. You can review the launches and activities of your competitors to come up with ideas but be sure to be unique and make it stand out. It should also be something that would appeal to your audience.

Your brand launch must be a priority. It requires thought and preparation. Deliberately plan the information that you desire to release and the timeline for when you plan to release it. You want your brand launch to leave a lasting impression on your target audience.

Activity 10 *Create an Internal and External Brand Launch Calendar.*	Create an internal and external calendar with a minimum of six months of execution and communication for both. Be sure to detail the communication methods that will be used and the timing of each. Below are a few examples of communications methods that can be used in a brand launch. • Email Communications • Social Media (Facebook, Twitter, LinkedIn, etc.) • Website updates • Television/Radio Advertisements • Displays/Signage • Collateral Updates (email signatures, letterhead, stationary) • Events

"The only man who behaves sensibly is my tailor; he takes my measurements anew every time he sees me, while all the rest go on with their old measurements and expect me to fit them."

George Bernard Shaw, Irish Playwright

Branding is a journey, not a destination. Your work does not end after you have developed your brand identity. You have to audit, evaluate, measure, report on and sometimes rebrand your brand. The organizations that have lasted for generations never get comfortable with how their brand is viewed by the public. Nor do they become complacent with how closely it is performing in relation to the brand mission and vision.

Auditing Your Brand

Maintaining a successful brand requires an ongoing effort and commitment to your brand story, vision and mission. It takes work to maintain brand standards and this work involves conducting health checks on your brand. Health checks are a means of ensuring your brand standards are upheld and they include monitoring results and reporting against goals. Successful brands must continually monitor the results of their branding efforts through routine health checks, known as brand audits.

> Successful brands must continually monitor the results of their branding efforts through routine health checks, known as brand audits.

A brand audit is a detailed analysis and review of how your brand is performing compared against its goals and its competitors. This audit will reveal the performance of your brand, it's strengths and weaknesses, as well as the audience perspective. Many large companies hire a branding agency to conduct these comprehensive audits. They normally provide an audit report which reviews both the internal and external branding. These reports are useful tools when considering a new branding strategy or rebrand. However, hiring a branding agency may not be affordable for many smaller organizations. Conducting your own brand audit may be more feasible and can still provide valuable information. There are a multitude of metrics that you can use to measure the performance of your brand, but there are some basis methods that any organization can use.

Using your brand mission and vision as your measuring stick, use the actions below, to audit the performance of your brand:

- **Survey Your Audience**
  The easiest way to review how your brand is performing is by directly surveying your audience. Surveys can be conducted by telephone, email, online or via paper questionnaires. There are several free and paid online sites that allow organizations to develop survey questions that can be emailed to your subscribed email list.

  Using a mixture of qualitative and quantitative questions about the customers interactions with each of your experience touchpoints will provide you with a clear view of how your brand is performing. You can even allow customers to write narrative statements about their experiences and rate their experiences at each of those touchpoints.

- **Review Your Web Analytics**
  Reviewing the traffic and activity on your website is another effective way to audit your brand performance. Most people conduct online research before they visit an organization or before they make a purchase, so the activity on your website will give you an idea of how interested people are in your brand. Web analytic services like Google Analytics and Yahoo Analytics will provide you with information on how people are finding your website, which pages they interact with the most and how much time they spend on your website. This information can be used to improve your website. It also can provide data regarding the demographic of people that use or visit your site.

Measuring Brand Awareness

People buy brands that they can remember, recall and that stand out in their minds. When they need laundry detergent, most people choose the brand that is most familiar to them. Name brand awareness influences our buying decisions more than the cost and effectiveness of the product. It is the way the human brain works. This is why brands should always be mindful of their target audiences awareness of their brand. Major brands spend great amounts of time, energy and resources on audience awareness, because it's so vital to their business operations. Having charitable events, concerts and even placing their names on stadiums and arenas are ways that major brands stimulate audience awareness of their brand.

> **Name brand awareness influences our buying decisions more than the cost and effectiveness of the product.**

Rebranding the Brand

The book of Genesis introduces us to a character by the name of Jacob. Early on, we learn that Jacob starts his brand off wrong. He steals the birthright from his older brother Esau by tricking his father and then runs away for twenty years. He immediately started his brand off as a thief and was known as such, for twenty years. However, God makes room for Jacob to experience a rebrand.

He spends almost twenty years rebuilding his brand, by working for his father-in-law, with the goal of marrying his youngest daughter Rachel. Jacob works tediously and with such excellence that at the end of his time working for his father-in-law, he leaves with two wives, many children and a vast amount of cattle and servants. After wrestling with an angel who changes his "brand" name from Jacob (which means "one who follows") to Israel (which means "one who rules"). Jacob continues to improve his brand perception by realizing that he must make amends with his brother,

> **Jacob experienced the ultimate rebrand.**

by returning home and begging for forgiveness. Jacob, now Israel, and his brother reconcile and he is no longer known as a thief, but a repentant man and a successful leader. Not only was his brand name changed, but his brand story was also changed. Jacob experienced the ultimate rebrand.

There are times when organizations that are already established have become known for something that does not adequately reflect the brand story that they wish to tell. It is in these moments where you may want to consider a rebrand.

Other reasons you may want to rebrand, include:
- Your brand needs to compete at more competitive level or in a new market.
- Your brand identity is dated.
- Your brand doesn't reflect your current brand story.
- Your brand has merged with another brand.
- Your brand has had legal difficulties.
- Your brand wishes to refocus its brand message.

Regardless of your reasons for rebranding, it is not uncommon but should be carefully considered and executed. Many companies would recommend different approaches to the rebranding process, but there are three baseline phases to the rebranding process.

The rebranding phases include:

- **Planning the Strategy**
  Before you jump right into color selection and logo design, you need to first plan a strategy for your brand. It's important to set goals, research the market opportunities, the competition, the audience you intend to reach and the changes that you need to make to the current brand. Reviewing your brand audit and comparing it to the competition will be helpful at this phase. You will also need to identify your brands key differentiators. Key

differentiators are the set of characteristics that set your organization apart from similar organizations in the marketplace (especially your main competitors).

- **Building the Brand**
  The next step is to build your brand. This should be done in logical order. You should first start with choosing a name and creating a tagline. From there you should design the logo and choose the color scheme. Lastly, you should design the website and other brand elements like stationary and other items.

- **Launching the Brand**
  The final phase in the rebranding process is launching the brand. A relaunch is a little different than new brand launch, because your brand has an established reputation and audience. The goal of a rebrand launch is to communicate to your current audience that your brand has changed. You must highlight the features that not only separate you from the competition, but you must also highlight the features that separate your brand from its past.

You are on your way to a successful brand. If you have been following this book from beginning to end to build your brand, remember that branding is a journey. Not a destination.

Congratulations, you have given birth to a living entity that has a personality and character. It is your responsibility to nurture its health and suability. Use this book a your guide map or "bible" for caring for your brand. Refer to it often and apply its principles as necessary. Whatever the future holds, be intentional about building a brand that can get there with you.

Activity 11

*Brand Audit
Checklist*

Answer this checklist objectively. Ask team members to give objective feedback as well.

1. Does everyone on your team know the brand's mission statement or vision?
2. Does your brand fulfill an unmet need that is not being served by the competition?
3. Are you connecting with your target audience weekly?
4. Can prospective website visitors easily find you online by searching your brand name?
5. Are your social media sites up-to-date? Is it an accurate reflection of your brand?
6. Does all your marketing materials look like its from the same company?
7. Are you optimizing your social media platforms to increase brand awareness?
8. Does your brand reflect your current brand story?

If you and your team members consistently answered, "No" to four or more questions, I would consider rebranding the brand. However, even if you answered, "Yes" to every question, continue routine health checks to ensure brand standards are upheld to avoid brand complacency.

"Without strategy, execution is aimless. Without execution, strategy is useless."

– Morris Chang, Founder of Taiwan Semiconductor Manufacturing Company

Glossary

Algorithms
Are a way of sorting posts in a user's feed based on relevancy to the user, instead of the time that it was posted.

Atmosphere
A business or organizations most dominant intellectual or emotional environment or attitude, that dictates experience.

Behavioral Patterns
The series of actions that a consumer follows before making a purchase.

Brand
A type of product manufactured by a particular company under a particular name.

Brand Ambassadors
The human representation of a brand and are responsible for socially promoting the organization.

Brand Identity
The method of visually communicating the values of your brand.

Brand Strategy
A plan that encompasses specific, long-term goals that can be achieved with the evolution of a successful brand.

Branding
The process of crafting the experiences and images you desire for people to have and remember when encountering your brand.

Color Harmony
The correct combination of colors that is attractive to the human eye.

Competitive Analysis
An evaluation of the strategic strengths and weaknesses of brands relative to your own product or service.

Culture
As the dominant pattern of learned and shared rules, beliefs, ideals and standards for shaping behavior, language, practices and understanding of a group of people.

Demographics
The statistical data and characteristics of a selected population.

Design Elements
Patterns and shapes that are used in materials such as merchandise packaging, presentations and fabrics.

Display Fonts
A category of typefaces used to grab the attention of the reader.

DPI
Dots Per Inch refers to the quantity of ink dots for every inch of a printed image.

Elevator Pitch
A short description of an idea, product, company or oneself, done in the time that it generally takes a person to get to their destination on an elevator.

Key Differentiator
The business attribute(s) that separates it from the competition in a particular marketplace.

Industry Influencer
An individual that has influence over potential customers in a specific industry.

Letterform Mark
The use of the first letter of the brand name, embellished enough to be distinctive and identifiable as an organization's logo.

Logos
Easily recognizable symbols or graphics that represents your brand.

Marketing
The exchanging offerings that have value for customers, clients, partners and society at large.

Offering
The total product or service offered to your customers, including availability, delivery technical support and quality.

Pantone
A system for matching colors, used in specifying printing inks.

Pictorial Marks
Symbols or shapes that represent a brand.

Pixelation
The visible display of individual pixels of in image.

Primary Colors
The three main colors of the color wheel that are then mixed with each other to create the secondary colors.

Product Demonstration
An exhibition of a products abilities to potential customers.

PPI
Pixels Per Inch indicates the number of pixels used for every inch of a digital image.

Resolution
Refers to the sharpness and clarity of an image.

Search Engine Optimization (SEO)
The process of including targeted keywords in your tags, titles and descriptions of any online content.

Secondary Color
A color resulting from the mixing of two primary colors.

Serifs
The small lines or strokes at the ends of font characters.

Stock Photos
A collection of photos, vectors, or illustrations that you can license by paying a fee or subscription to the author, to use the images in a variety of ways.

Social Media Algorithms
The codes embedded into most popular social media platforms, that attempt to predict what their users like and enjoy viewing, based on their previous online activity.

Sub-Brands
Brands owned and closely tied to a larger parent company or original brand, but are still brands with their own identity.

Target Audience
A specific group of people, identified as the intended recipients of a message.

Tertiary Colors
The color result of blending primary and secondary colors together.

Touch-Point
Every potential point of interaction a customer has with a brand.

Trademark
A legal filing that protects words, names, symbols and logos that distinguish your brand.

Typography
The art and technique of arranging type to make written language legible, readable and appealing when displayed.

Uniform Resource Locator (URL)
The address or location of a resource on the internet.

Unique Selling Proposition (USP)

The factor or consideration presented by a seller as the reason that one product or service is different from and better than that of the competition.

Utility

The value or benefit a customer receives from a business exchange.

Vison Session

A meeting with a group of stakeholders that involves asking the group to appraise the current state of the organization and where they realistically expect to be in the future.

Vlog

A blog where the content and postings are primarily in video form.

Webinars

Online seminars.

Wordmark

A text-only design for the logo representation of an organization.